The Politics of U

The Politics of Urban Governance

Also by Jon Pierre

Governance, Politics and the State (*with B. Guy Peters*)

Governing Complex Societies (*with B. Guy Peters*)

Partnerships in Urban Governance

The Politics of Urban Governance

Jon Pierre

palgrave
macmillan

First published 2011 by
PALGRAVE MACMILLAN

Palgrave Macmillan in the UK is an imprint of Macmillan Publishers Limited, registered in England, company number 785998, of Houndmills, Basingstoke, Hampshire RG21 6XS.

Palgrave Macmillan in the US is a division of St Martin's Press LLC, 175 Fifth Avenue, New York, NY 10010.

Palgrave Macmillan is the global academic imprint of the above companies and has companies and representatives throughout the world.

Palgrave® and Macmillan® are registered trademarks in the United States, the United Kingdom, Europe and other countries.

ISBN 978–0–333–73267–0   hardback
ISBN 978–0–333–73268–7   paperback

This book is printed on paper suitable for recycling and made from fully managed and sustained forest sources. Logging, pulping and manufacturing processes are expected to conform to the environmental regulations of the country of origin.

A catalogue record for this book is available from the British Library.

A catalog record for this book is available from the Library of Congress.

10   9   8   7   6   5   4   3   2   1
20   19   18   17   16   15   14   13   12   11

Printed in China

Contents

Acknowledgements

This book project was for several years 'the other project', a tempting, but also luring and uncertain academic endeavour outside the realm of the more routine and inescapable writing projects. Although much of my work the past years has been in other areas of political science, urban governance never stopped intriguing me. When I joined the Department of Government at the University of Strathclyde in the mid-1990s, Gerry Stoker inspired me to recast much of urban research into the urban governance framework. With Guy Peters, my governance research took a somewhat broader approach and it has been intriguing to see how easily much of that work translates into urban political analysis. Guy, as ever, has been a source of never-failing support and encouragement. The comments of Patrick Le Galès and Clarence Stone on a previous draft were integral to the completion of the book. At Palgrave Macmillan, Steven Kennedy, with a characteristic combination of carrots, sticks and sermons, has pushed this project along. In addition, the research for this book has benefited from discussions about governance over the years with Ole Johan Andersen, Susan Clarke, Alan Harding, Dennis Judd, Asbjörn Röiseland, Rod Rhodes and Jeff Sellers. My sincere thanks to you all. That said, the usual disclaimer that all remaining errors in the text are my responsibility applies.

There has, however, been one temptation that I have been unable to resist. Monika, Miranda and Jonathan Pierre have successfully conspired to convince me that there are matters outside the office far more rewarding than any academic spoil. This book is for them.

Gothenburg, Sweden   JON PIERRE

Chapter 1

Why Study Urban Politics?

This is a book about how cities are governed, about the importance of institutions in urban governance and about the different goals cities prioritize. The book pursues an argument reaffirming the position of institutional theory in urban politics as a means of uncovering the structural and normative underpinnings of urban governance.

Urban politics is city politics. It defines and regulates how the city should be organized, how it should allocate its resources and how – and by whom – it should be governed. Central government policies play an important role in providing well-being for the citizens of a country but in many countries it is local authorities that make most of the key decisions related to welfare and public service. When we say 'city politics' it is with the understanding that urban politics strictly speaking refers to politics at the local level.

This chapter gives a brief introduction to the book. It presents urban politics as a field of study and introduces urban governance and institutional theory.

Urban politics

The first question to address is: why should we bother ourselves with urban politics? There are obvious reasons for us as citizens to understand who makes the essential decisions shaping the city we live in and perhaps to try to influence those decisions. As citizens we should be concerned about urban politics because most of the decisions that shape our existence tend to be made at the local level. Also, many of us tend to be most concerned about issues closest to us. There are other reasons for us as social scientists to do research on urban politics.

1

The literature offers a couple of clues to this issue. Urban politics, writes Clarence Stone (2008: 285), 'is a matter of understanding how a changing mix of forces is related to an evolving urban condition'. Cryptic as this may sound, Stone's argument is that urban politics is about the confluence of economic, social and political forces and how they shape city life. Urban politics offers a more direct and more visible manifestation of these forces and how they shape a public space and collective action, compared to the level of the nation state.

Peter John (2008) suggests that urban politics has two important advantages to most other areas of political science: propinquity and numerosity. Propinquity 'denotes the closeness of the urban space where actors interact and tend to be small in number' (John 2008: 21). In urban politics, distance – whether between electors and elected or between bureaucrats and clients – is always small and the immediate nature and visibility of policy choices provides an understanding of the role of politics in shaping society.

Numerosity means that there are multiple cases to be studied within the same national context. The researcher can survey local governments in a country and use statistical methods to uncover relationships between, for instance, political and economic variables that are not detectable in qualitative analyses, let alone case studies. More importantly, perhaps, this research can be conducted with control for variables that are known to explain common political-science phenomena, such as political culture, economic variables and welfare indicators. By comparing policy choice in local authorities in a country, those variables are controlled for since they affect all local authorities similarly or roughly similarly.

The intriguing image of urban politics is thus that it matters, it is easily researchable and it lends itself to a variety of methods. True, there is less drama and appeal about urban politics than that which surrounds the politics of global warming or the fight against terrorism, but it still has much to offer in terms of contextual richness and understanding politics at a close distance. For nothing else, a bus ticket is cheaper than an airline ticket, as Peter John argues (John 2008).

Urban politics is to considerable degree shaped by the national context in which it is embedded. Every national environment has its own specific institutional arrangements, its own national policy towards cities, its own political culture and tends to foster its own urban political economy and types of urban regimes. This makes comparative analysis and theory building difficult (Ashford 1975, Denters and Rose 2005, DiGaetano 2006, Keating 1991, Pierre 2005). However, urban politics has always been rich in theory (Judge *et al*. 1995, Davies and Imbroscio 2008) and while those theories appear, as theories, to be applicable to cities in almost all national settings, they are more reflective of the context which they draw upon than is often realized. This theoretical ethnocentricity explains why there occur 'misfits' when the theory is applied to local government in other national contexts (Davies 2003, Harding 1995). Theory does not travel as well as is sometimes assumed, particularly not theories on urban politics.

The research field of urban politics is defined by a particular institutional level, the local level. Thus, it is not defined in relation to any particular theory. This has helped make urban politics as a field of academic enquiry much more inter-disciplinary than most other social-science research fields. While urban politics has a natural kinship with political science, it is also closely related to sociology, geography and economics. Since urban politics is concerned with issues like what shapes urban policy choice; or what accounts for differences in life chances in different parts of a city; or the tensions between different strategies of urban planning and land use, urban politics has few problems in incorporating variables which typically speak to sociology or economics or geography.

Urban politics has for long been an established subfield of political science but the prominence of that subfield has varied considerably across time and space. In the United States in the 1960s and 1970s, urban politics was 'hot' (Orr and Johnson 2008). This was when most of the salient issues in political science were urban politics issues, as was the case with the debate among pluralists and elite theorists at that time (Dahl 1961, Hunter 1953, Polsby 1963). But the American local authorities suffer from limited autonomy and institutional fragmentation (Keating 1991). When federal policies and programmes towards the cities declined and, finally, all but disappeared in the 1980s and 1990s, urban politics both as a research field and a practice experienced a similar decline (Orr and Johnson 2008). There was a significant rediscovery of the urban political scene with Clarence Stone's seminal book *Regime Politics* (Stone 1989) and urban regime theory has been a leitmotif in US urban politics for much of the 1990s and 2000s.

The European experience paints a rather different picture. Political mobilization is higher in Europe, local authorities are comparatively speaking more resourceful and the political discourse is shaped by ideology to a much higher degree than in the United States. As a result, urban politics did not experience the same decline as in the United States. In the 1980s when American urban politics was clearly in decline, European cities in most countries (with the UK as an important exception) were doing relatively well (see Le Galès 2002). Thus, urban politics was an exciting research field and remains very much a dynamic subfield of political science.

On both sides of the Atlantic, the rapidly growing interest in public management reform during the past couple of decades has to some extent redefined the urban politics agenda. With Ronald Reagan in the US and Mrs Thatcher and John Major, then Tony Blair in the UK leading or pursuing the public management campaign which played out to a large extent at the local level where public services are delivered, urban managerialism in different guises has become a significant part of urban politics (see Chapter 3). The focus on managerial issues has been so strong that it has almost crowded out more traditional urban politics traditional issues like urban planning, policy choice and the extent to which 'politics matters' (Sharpe and Newton 1984).

American urban politics research has been criticized for being driven by fads and political agendas (Jones 1989: 35):

[W]hen there are riots in cities, we write much about social justice, the entrance of new participants, and racial discrimination. When cities cannot balance their budgets, the fiscal crisis literature gets a boost. When city economies are in the doldrums, books on economic development appear.

The interest in current affairs and issues is largely a valid account of urban politics not only in the US but also in much of Europe. However, urbanists are not entirely focused on current developments; in both America and Europe much energy has been also devoted to develop various theories of urban politics and urban governance (see Judge *et al.* 1995).

From urban politics to urban governance

Urban politics in many countries is now gradually turning towards urban governance. This process began in the 1990s along with a growing interest in 'governance' more broadly among academics, practitioners and politicians, not least in Britain (Rhodes 1996, Stoker 1998). Governance, unlike 'government', looks at the interplay between state and society and the extent to which collective projects can be achieved through a joint public and private mobilization of resources. Politically, this means that the public sector does not have to deliver all public services itself; it can coordinate service production among public actors at different institutional levels, private actors, NGOs and other potential participants. Academically, governance initially redirects attention from institutions to processes and from the exercise of political and legal authority to public entrepreneurship and public–private partnership. This was usually described as a 'shift from government to governance'; an unfortunate choice of words as government continued to play a key, albeit changed role in the provision of services. Furthermore, outside the UK many countries had had long experiences with different forms of institutionalized interaction between the state and actors in its environment and could not understand the novelty of this arrangement or the purported 'shift'. Rather, what had changed was the role of government in governance (Pierre and Peters 2000).

Governance in this gestalt fits perfectly with the research agenda in urban politics where public–private partnerships and other forms of exchange between local authorities and their environment had long been in place. Thus, urban governance offered a theory or perspective to describe the exercise of political authority in the city and the possibilities and perils associated with different forms of public–private interaction.

In Chapter 2 we discuss urban governance at some length. Before we proceed to that discussion we must briefly discuss how institutions fit into the process-oriented nature of governance.

Institutions and governance: an odd couple, perhaps

We began this chapter with saying that the overall purpose of the book is to show the contribution of institutional theory in the study of urban governance. How do institutions blend with governance conceived of a process of blending public and private resources?

Again, we will discuss this issue at length in the next chapter. For now, we must note that the concept of institution has multiple meanings in institutional theory. One meaning is structure, organization; institutions represent organizational continuity and define the range of choice and behaviour of the organization's members. The second meaning of institution is norm, value, rules and practices. This is obviously a more subtle and less tangible interpretation of institution, but rules, values and norms constrain behaviour just as much as structure or organization does. Thus, what holds together the two meanings of institution is that they both 'shape and constrain' (Thelen and Steinmo 1991) social behaviour. Most importantly, institutional theory looks at the interplay between these two meanings, that is, how structures become carriers of social norms and values and how those norms and values become institutionalized (see Peters 1999).

With this brief elaboration of institution it should be clear that there are no inconsistencies between institution and governance. Both meanings of institution are relevant to the study of governance. Political structures are important players in the governance process since they define collective goals and coordinate public and private efforts towards those goals. Institution in the more abstract sense matters too; as this book will show, different norms and values defined as governance goals shape much of what actors can contribute towards those goals.

* * *

No single book can cover urban governance in all countries of the world, either conceptually or empirically. The purpose of this text is to describe different models of governance with regard to the objectives of that governance. Therefore, the issue of which countries are included becomes less important than if the book had been more empirically oriented. The main empirical models for the analysis of urban politics as a practice and as a field of research are the UK and the United States. There are numerous comparative observations from other national contexts like Scandinavia and Southeast Asia, but most of the analysis covers urban governance in the former two countries. Governance as described in the models will play out differently in different national contexts; pro-growth governance in Italy will, perhaps, be differently organized and conducted than similar governance in Finland. Hopefully the book will serve as a framework or a catalyst for more in-depth empirical research on urban governance in different types of national contexts so that the broader theoretical perspective can be confronted with empirically rich studies.

Furthermore, it almost goes without saying that there are many aspects of urban politics and governance which have not been given due attention in the book. The urban setting is not reserved for benevolent and civilized human interaction. It is also the scene for public disorder, riots, crime, homelessness and surveillance, all of which are issues high on the contemporary political agenda in many countries

(Coleman 2004, Crawford 1999, 2002, Waddington *et al.* 1989). Important as these issues certainly are they are only discussed very briefly in the book.

Organization of the book

The remainder of the book is organized as follows. Chapter 2 elaborates the analyses of urban governance and institutional theory and shows how the two theoretical perspectives can be integrated. In Chapters 3–6 four different models of urban governance are elaborated: managerial governance, corporatist governance, pro-growth governance and welfare governance. These four models depart from four different overarching objectives of urban governance. Each model is assessed in terms of its goals objectives, instruments and outcomes.

Chapters 7 and 8 approach urban politics from a different point of departure compared to the four models. Chapter 7, 'The Decline of Urban Politics?', presents an elaborated discussion about overarching recent changes in urban politics in most western countries. The first section deals with the changing cast of actors in urban politics, whereas the second section addresses the changing urban political agenda. These two developments are obviously closely related; new issues bring in new actors and similarly new forms of political participation help put new issues on the political agenda. Thus, emerging forms of social movements and citizen protest will be discussed alongside the changing character of urban political issues such as environmental protection, migration and the sustainability of cities in light of these powerful changes. Following this discussion, the chapter looks at the changing role of professionals in urban politics and city administration. These groups seek to insulate their areas from political guidance so that professional norms can dictate the design of city services. These groups offer powerful resistance against cutbacks in public spending and thus pose a significant challenge to the urban political elite. The chapter closes with a discussion concerning the extent to which the current 'managerialism', coupled with the other developments described in the chapter, under-cuts the traditional role of elected officials in urban politics and what scope of policy choice actually exists for the urban political elite. Issues related to control and accountability will be discussed in this section.

Chapter 8, 'Cities in Global Governance', is devoted to an analysis of the challenges to urban governance that the recent internationalization of cities poses. One important conse-quence of such internationalization is that it tends to detach private businesses from the local political economy. Also, enhancing international networks – for example, in the con-text of the EU – frequently creates conflict between those who advocate primary concern with the 'truly' local issues such as social welfare. The chapter also looks at what drives cities to position themselves as international actors and the local consequences of such strategies in a more general perspective. Obviously, this chapter also discusses the role of the nation state in these processes and the role of the EU in its direct exchange with cities and regions.

Finally, Chapter 9, 'Conclusions: The Future of Urban Poli-tics', discusses the analytical utility of the models discussed in the book. The role of local government in these different mod-els of urban governance is assessed. Also, the chapter discusses how tensions between different models of urban governance cause 'ungovernability' or 'governance gaps' in urban politics. An important conclusion of the analysis is that no city displays all characteristics of any single model of urban governance. The chapter concludes with a more general discussion about possible future directions of urban politics and urban govern-ance, given the previously discussed changes among actors and issues and the growing international complexities in which cities increasingly often find themselves.

Chapter 2

The Challenge of Urban Governance

Institutional analysis became a dominant theoretical perspective in political science in the early 1990s and showed convincingly that institutions, both in terms of organizational structure and as norms and values, are essential to understanding governance and political behaviour. At about the same time, institutional theory made important inroads in economics when Douglass North, the 1993 Nobel Prize laureate in economics, showed that actors in markets tend to use routines and simple rules rather than utility-maximizing strategies to make their decisions (North 1990). Whether in politics or markets, the institutional argument states that actors certainly have goals but the pursuit of those goals is embedded in, and constrained by, systems of rules, meanings and values, and 'the organizational dimension of politics' (March and Olsen 1989). If political analysis can uncover those underlying norms and values about what politics should be all about we are well under way to a deeper understanding of political and social behaviour.

This was the basic argument of institutional theory which mainstream political science embraced. In urban politics – particularly American urban politics – institutional theory never became as prominent as in other areas of political science. American urban politics was primarily concerned with studies of urban elites and regimes and the politics of economic development (Stone 2008). In Europe there was a greater interest in the organizational dimension of urban politics, including intergovernmental relationships and the party politics in local government. Even so, however, institutional theory never became as prominent in defining the research agenda as it did in most other areas of political science. Thus, ironically, attention to institutions left urban politics at almost the same time as it developed into the perhaps dominating research field in other areas of political science (Peters 1999, Peters and Pierre 2007). It has not been until a few years into the twenty-first century that urbanists have rediscovered what mainstream political scientists found in the 1990s; that institutions are critical to an understanding of governance and political phenomena more broadly.

This was also a time when globalization caught momentum, exposing countries and cities to the thrust of deregulated international capital. By a similar irony urban political economy all but disappeared at the time when it was becoming increasingly clear that the prosperity of cities depended in large parts on economic factors. Globalization represented a new set of economic contingencies for many cities whose industry had previously been protected by national borders but which now found themselves exposed to international competition. This new economic pressure was particularly felt in cities in Central and Eastern Europe and triggered an unprecedented shockwave of structural change, plant closures, mass unemployment and loss of social benefits. In the western world, too, economic globalization triggered processes of profound economic restructuring. But, while this could have been the heyday of research on urban political economy and the subordination of policy choice to economic forces, surprisingly little research was conducted on those processes.

Again, American and European urbanists chose partially different paths. The Americans tended to see local economic development mainly as an endogenous process to the city and therefore focused on the role of political values and the extent to which there was any scope for policy choice in the process of economic restructuring (Mollenkopf 1983, Peterson 1981, Stone and Sanders 1987). Meanwhile, most European urbanists saw the economic challenges facing cities as a restructuring of the capitalist economy (see, for instance, Duncan and Goodwin 1982, 1985, 1988, King 1987).

We need to be aware of the different trajectories that urban politics in America and Europe have followed. In the US, 'in the 1950s and into the 1970s, urban politics was hot' (Orr and Johnson 2008: 3). It had a strong niche in political science and hosted many of the leading scholars in the discipline. In the 1990s, US urban politics declined on most measures (Orr and Johnson 2008). In Europe, meanwhile, urban politics remained a strong and dynamic subsection of political science. This is not the place to dwell on what explains this difference. American political science has had a major influence on the development in Europe during much of the twentieth century and the decline in the US, which shaped the urban politics literature, stood ast odds with the more positive development of the research field in Europe.

The book develops institutional theory in the field of urban politics. It is an institutional theory of urban politics and urban governance which shows how norms, goals and values form the urban political agenda and the structural framework within which it is pursued. It offers a perspective on urban politics which will improve our understanding of urban policy choice, of the pursuit of economic growth and of the rearticulation of the urban space in a globalized world.

Cities and urban governance

'By itself, the city becomes the prestige symbol for the whole civilization', wrote once the famous American urbanist Lewis Mumford (1938: 233). It is difficult to imagine recurrent meetings of groups of people and of political, social, cultural and economic exchange or, indeed, a civilized society without some agglomeration of structures and services surrounding it. To Mumford, a city represented a social fabric where the opinions and preferences of individuals are translated into public, collective action. Urban spaces – shaped and reshaped by political choice embedded in institutional and economic power fields (DiGaetano 2006, Kohn 2004, Magnusson 1996) – around the world offer forums for political debate, culture in any form and shape, commerce, churches, education, work and leisure. It is difficult to think of civilization, in the original meaning of the word, in geographical settings with few inhabitants. Civilization requires people, and people dwell in cities.

If cities are civilization, however, they are also economic, social and political creatures. Historically, cities were located along trade paths or where national security interests dictated that defence facilities should be concentrated. Later, cities grew up where industry found favourable locations close to exploitable natural resources. Thus, unlike most nation states, the origin of cities is not ethnic, cultural, or geographic but mostly economic. The trajectory of urban economic development is supplemented by the role of cities in shaping civilization. As democracy emerged, cities became the key arena for participation and political involvement, whereas democracy at the level of the nation state became concerned with issues on how to create effective governance and appropriate political institutions. There was some beauty in the small scale of local democracy in the small towns and municipalities. 'Kingdoms and Republics are man-made, but Townships seem to spring from the hands of God', wrote de Tocqueville (quoted in Goldsmith 1992) when reflecting on the role of local institutions in American democracy. In a similar vein, John Stuart Mill saw local democracy as critical to democracy at the level of the nation state since it is at the local level that people are offered an opportunity to engage in democratic debate and practices (see Hill 1974).

That having been said, cities have always been more diverse and heterogeneous than merely serving as political arenas, and political institutions have been far from sovereign in shaping the urban landscape (Hall 1988, Soja 2000). To be sure, many urbanists – both those coming from a Marxist perspective and those with a market-based view on urban politics – insist that local politics is invariably subordinate to the economic powers that rest in globalization processes and economic restructuring. Others identify migration and social change as the chief forces challenging urban political institutions. For all their disagreement on most other issues, these observers of urban civilization and urban politics agree on at least one basic idea, namely that just as cities are much more than local authorities, so is urban governance a process encompassing the greater urban space and not just the institutions of local government.

If, thus, the history of cities has much to tell us about how governance has been organized and provided in different political and economic contexts, it is only a very slight exaggeration to suggest that over the past couple of decades urban politics in the western democracies has changed paradigmatically. The historical emphasis on local democracy and public services has been replaced by objectives related to enhancing efficiency, cost-awareness, customerization of services and the inclusion of the voluntary sector into public-service production and delivery. To promote those objectives, cities throughout the western world have seen a whole array of new instruments being introduced, such as contracting out, privatization, public–private partnerships and 'third-sector' solutions.

Urban politics, broadly speaking, has become less concerned with the management and accommodation of political conflict and more concerned with management thinking, efficiency assessments, private-sector-inspired models of service production and joint public–private mobilization of resources. In other words, there has been a shift in attention from designing the local institutional arrangement in ways that promote participation and debate to a focus on urban governance.

The study of urban politics has changed accordingly, albeit along different paths in the United States and Europe. Previously, much of American urban politics described how cities and their elected officials related to private businesses and how they managed their dependency to private investment. Now, the focus is gradually shifting from a somewhat narrow focus on the relationship between the corporate and political elites in a city – the key focus of urban regime theory (Stone 1989) – towards what Stone (2008: 300) calls 'alternative lenses' to observe urban politics, such as a more inclusive analysis of the governance of cities. In Europe, urban regime theory was seen as an abstraction of American urban political economy and was never embraced by urbanists. As Alan Harding (1995: 46–7) points out, there is a 'powerful tradition of skepticism among UK political scientists about imported US theories and methods ... US approaches are generally dismissed as insensitive to fundamental differences between the two countries'. In a similar vein, Jonathan Davies argues that since urban regimes are not likely to emerge in the UK, political, economic and institutional context regime theory is not a useful analytical model in Britain (Davies 2003).

This book puts forward an institutional approach to urban politics to explain (cross-national and intra-national) differences in the organization of cities and differences in the agendas that cities pursue. There have been precious few studies of the institutional dimension of urban politics (but see Clarke 1995, Lowndes 2001, 2008, Pierre 1999, Sellers 2001). This is both unfortunate and frustrating, given the advances of institutional analysis in almost all other subfields of political science (Pierre *et al.* 2008). Institutions prescribe certain types of social action and embody collective values and norms. Once we understand the institutions, we also understand much about policy choice and political behaviour. Let us now look more closely at these institutions.

Institutions in urban politics

Institutions matter significantly in urban politics and they do so in two different ways. First of all, local political institutions – the structures of the local authority – remain the pillars which sustain and embody political authority. To be sure, it is difficult to conceive of representative government at any institutional level without institutions. Much of recent reform, such as the creation of various forms of partnerships or informal networks with third-sector organizations, has aimed at enhancing the city's 'capacity to act' (Stone 1989); it also tends to blur the role of formal political institutions. However, although we may find them rigid and old fashioned, we do not yet have any viable alternatives to councils and executive boards when it comes to providing citizens with opportunities to influence city politics or to hold those elected to democratic account.

Indeed, it could well be argued that the growing significance of non-elected actors in urban politics in many countries only increases the need for political control and accountability. Holding informal networks or partnerships to political account is not an option since they were never elected in the first place. Similarly, the recent debate on various forms of 'stakeholderism' has not been able to come up with a distinct and sustainable model for democratic input and accountability. Thus, as long as we think that citizens' input and electoral accountability matter, representative institutions remain critical to democratic governance at the urban level. Whether we like them or not, we are – for the time being at least – stuck with the traditional representative political institutions.

Second, institutions matter also in a more abstract sense. Institutional theory argues that institutions should be conceived of as structures or as systems of norms, recurrent patterns of behaviour, rules, practices and systems of meaning and beliefs. Applied to urban politics, this aspect of institutions is not concerned with the configuration of the local political system but rather with the overarching objectives of urban politics. These abstract institutions are related to symbols, collective history and memories, and values. They tell us much about 'what kind of city this is' and what its population wants it to be (March and Olsen 1989). Anyone who visits a city for the first time will be told tales about the history of the city and its prominent inhabitants. Such collective memories and myths define much of what the city is today and what it wants to be tomorrow. These abstract values and norms are institutions because they guide individual and collective action. Thus, in order to understand the governance in any given city we should ask questions such as: what norms and objectives guide local authorities? Which political, social and economic actors have defined those objectives, and who benefits from them? To what extent have those norms and goals become institutionalized at the local level of the political system?

Institutional theory also argues that an analysis of the relationship between these two aspects of institutions – between structures and norms – tells us much about the political priorities of cities. Cities that seem to define their role as primarily catering to private businesses will have a different structural design compared to cities who have made social justice and distributive policies their main concern. Urban policy choice is thus embedded in a structural framework that allows or facilitates some choices more than others. These structures are manifestations of core values and norms in the urban politics which – to borrow an oft-cited phrase from Katherine Thelen and Sven Steinmo (1991: 10) – 'shape and constrain' urban political and social behaviour. The key reason why institutional theory has a dual focus on structure as well as systems or norms, routines, practices and recurrent patterns of behaviour (in addition to the relationship between structure and norm) is precisely because they both define what is appropriate behaviour. Also, structure and norm tend to reinforce each other; political structures created to deliver some kind of public service tend to promote those services and explain to the public why they are important.

The remainder of the chapter is organized as follows. We will first briefly introduce the theory and concept of governance which we then apply more specifically to urban politics. After that, the chapter discusses the role of institutions in urban governance. The chapter closes with a presentation of four models of urban governance, derived from four different clusters of norms, objectives and values in urban politics.

Theories of governance

Governance has become somewhat of a conceptual fad in almost any social-science analytical context during the 1990s and 2000s. A number of forces have propelled this development (see Pierre and Peters 2000, Rhodes 1996, Stoker 1998); the development towards a minimalist (or regulatory) state; administrative reform emphasizing managerial autonomy and a lower profile for elected politicians; cutbacks in the public sector; and a growing critique and cynicism among voters, just to mention a few. Perhaps most importantly, governance has emerged as an alternative to the state-centric model of service delivery. Here, the general argument is that the state (or political institutions more broadly) does not necessarily have to produce and deliver all services itself; the important thing is that they are delivered. The main roles of political institutions in this governance perspective is to make collective priorities and goals, while the pursuit of those goals is conducted in concert with a broad variety of societal actors such as organized interests, civil society and private business.

This development is sometimes referred to as 'a shift' from government to governance. Such a 'shift', it is argued in the more extreme versions of the argument, has created a 'new governance', which is a model of 'governing without government' (Rhodes 1996, 1997). For all its pedagogical appeals, the model presents a view of modern society as governed by self-organizing networks with little or no real power left for political institutions and representative government. However, even a casual glance around the western world suggests that governments remain very much at the centre of governance. Recent reforms to introduce new models of governance tend, for the most part, to be initiated and implemented by those institutions, as was, for instance, the case of the so-called economic regions in the UK. Political institutions still control vast financial resources and significant political power, and so we need to reconsider if what is happening really is a 'shift' from government to governance or if it, in fact, is a matter of redefining the role of government in governance.

It is also difficult to see the novelty in state–society exchanges, dialogue and joint ventures. Most European countries have a long tradition with various forms of corporatism, which portrays the state in constant dialogue with organized societal interests (see Migdal 2001, 2004). Again, the governance we have seen emerging during the 1990s has changed that picture somewhat but the important point is that bringing societal actors into the process of public service delivery is not a very recent phenomenon.

There are also normative and ideological aspects of the concept of governance that need to be separated from governance as an object of academic study. Simone Gross and Hambleton critically observe that, to some, governance 'is less a creative process for solving societal problems than a mechanism for allowing the state to abdicate its responsibilities for providing social care and support' and that 'governance in the absence of strong government can lead to urban breakdown' (Simone Gross and Hambleton 2007: 9). Again, there has been less of a 'shift from government to governance' than a change in the role of government in governance.

Together with Guy Peters, I developed a typology of governance models (Pierre and Peters 2005). Ranging from state-centric governance to 'governing without government', this typology highlights different models of societal involvement in the process of governing society. Space does not allow a more lengthy discussion on these aspects of governance. The important observation is that the notion of a 'shift' from government to governance fails to take into account the many different dimensions of governance, such as which structures or agents define collective goals, mobilize resources, provide information about societal changes and so on. From this perspective, we see that what is changing is first and foremost the roles of government in governance. It is clear that government plays a different role in governance today, compared to a couple of decades ago, but it is equally clear that even today government is a key actor – if not *the* key actor – in governance.

This discussion speaks directly to urban governance as well. The role of political institutions and actors in urban governance tends to be seen as both embedded in complex contingencies with private capital and also captive of national and regional institutional structures. Thus, many of the issues that are currently seen as novelties at the level of the nation state have defined urban governance for a very long period of time. At the local level, there has probably always existed a need to mobilize resources not just from political sources but also from all actors in the urban territory in order to pursue collective goals. As a result, urban political institutions are probably less overwhelmed by 'new governance' practices than most national institutions.

Understanding urban governance

The book elaborates an institutional theory of urban politics by opening up a multitude of urban political objectives and showing how those objectives become translated into institutional structures. More specifically, we outline an institutional framework for the analysis of urban governance. The governance perspective on urban politics is focused on different models of public–private exchange and concerted resource mobilization. The governance approach suggests a shift in analytical focus from government towards governance. This shift implies less attention to formal structures of local government and instead a focus on the processes through which cities relate to their environment, for instance in public service delivery. Governance could be defined as processes through which public and private resources are coordinated in the pursuit of collective interests. Thus, as a concept, governance is more encompassing and broad than government. Government can play different roles in governance, ranging from being the key coordinator to merely operating as one of several public and private organizations in some jointly defined and executed project (Stoker 1998).

Governance has quickly become a catchword in urban political studies in a large number of countries. In Britain, the past decade has seen a booming interest in urban governance among academic observers (see, for instance, Buck *et al.* 2005, Stoker 2000). The focus on governance has also been propelled by the Blair government's emphasis on governance at all institutional levels and a shift from a state-centred society towards partnerships and inclusion. Indeed, the British 2000 Local Government Act places a statutory duty on local authorities to develop 'community strategies', describing how the authority will engage NGOs, civil society and other societal actors in the process of governance and public-service delivery. In the United States, governance is viewed mainly as inter-governmental coordination in metropolitan areas, although there is a strong historical interest in various forms of public–private partnerships, too (Beauregard 1998; see also Stone 2008). In Australia and New Zealand, finally, the New Public Management reforms have highlighted alternative forms of service production and closer cooperation between private business and local government. The New Public Management model of public administration should not be confused with governance, although there is some kinship between the two models – for instance, in terms of how they portray the relationship between the public and private sectors in society (Peters and Pierre 1998).

If one of the differences between 'government' and governance is that the latter perspective is more concerned with processes while the former revolves around structures and institutions, the institutional dimension of governance easily gets lost in the array of networks, partnerships and joint ventures. However, as pointed out earlier, institutions matter, both in very concrete terms such as representative institutions and in the more abstract sense where institutions refer to overarching norms, beliefs and ideas about the role of politics in society. Both types of institutions are critical to structure the local political discourse. It is true that the governance perspective on urban politics downplays attention to structures, but that does not mean that they disappear or lose significance altogether. When we say that we want to bring in the institutional dimension of urban governance it means that we will look at the role of formal institutional structures in governance and what values, norms and objectives shape urban governance.

Along these theoretical paths of arguing, this book develops two themes, both of which relate to the institutional dimension of urban politics. Normative institutional theory argues that the two aspects of institutions – structures and systems of norms, beliefs, practices and routines – are inseparable and play key roles in reinforcing each other and in shaping political and social behaviour (Peters 1999). This book looks at this interplay between structures and values in urban governance. Thus, the first argument developed in the book is that the focus on process in the current governance literature overlooks the significance of those systems of values and norms which give these processes meaning and purpose. Indeed, we cannot understand and assess governance as a process without studying the purposes, goals and objectives which sustain and direct the process. These overarching values will be approached as institutions in the way neo-institutional theory defines them. Thus, the book describes different institutional models of urban governance, some of which are potentially in conflict with each other whereas other models are more complementary. Each model will be outlined in a separate chapter and assessed in terms of its objectives, instruments and outcomes.

Institutions in urban governance

The second theme of the book is the significance of institutions in urban politics and governance and the need to bring in institutional theory in urban politics. The book shows how thinking about local government and governance in an institutional perspective brings out a number of intriguing perspectives which add considerably to our understanding of urban governance. One example is the consequences of organizational fragmentation in cities. From an institutional perspective, such fragmentation can be seen as contending forms of governance among different segments of the city administration; local economic development offices are heavily engaged in pro-growth governance, while social workers relate to their external environment in ways more akin to professional governance. These tensions between different segments of the city in turn help explain what is sometimes referred to as 'ungovernability of cities' or 'governance gaps' (Pierce 1993).

Applying an institutional perspective to urban governance rests on the assumption that structure matters; despite the powerful influence of economic and societal actors on urban political decision-making, urban political institutions remain the only effective linkage between the populace and elected officials. Although these institutions tend to lack the leverage to resolve these issues, democratic local government can only be accomplished so long as political institutions matter. This is not to suggest that the focus on urban political institutions is based entirely on normative ideas and wishful thinking; since we want urban politics to be democratic we assume – and hope – that elective and representative institutions really play a significant role in shaping urban policy choice. As mentioned earlier, much of the research on these issues during the 1990s, particularly in the United States, has drawn on urban regime theory (Stone 1989). Urban regimes are coalitions of political and economic actors and interests centred around policy objectives of economic growth and development. One of the key questions in this literature has been the extent to which 'politics matters', that is, the capacity of political actors to impose collective preferences on policy choice despite the presence of powerful economic interests. The general pattern emerging from this body of literature suggests that political actors are capable of shaping the development of a city according to policy preferences, although policy choice is deeply embedded in economic structures (see, for example, Stone and Sanders 1987, Jones and Bachelor 1986).

One of the main challenges to urban governance rests in the circumstance that the levers controlled by cities are far inferior to the forces that threaten social cohesion and the long-term prosperity of the city. Changes in the economic and social systems in society tend to manifest themselves most distinctly at the urban level. Structural changes in the economy can be powerful enough to destroy the entire social fabric of the local society (see Hoerr 1988).

In a similar albeit less dramatic way, changes in central government policy can have far-reaching consequences for individual cities and regions. This applies, for instance, to policies which support certain technologies or international exchanges or educational programmes. The state may or may not choose to compensate cities that end up losing in the allocation of financial resources; in fact, central government in several countries today encourages competition among cities in order to increase the quality of public services. It is often argued that the state mitigates the impact of globalization on cities (Beauregard 1995), but the extent to which that is the case varies considerably among different countries. Immigration policy poses a tremendous challenge to local authorities in most major cities in Europe, but the issue of who should carry the financial burden for the implementation of immigration policy is often negotiated and renegotiated between the state and the cities. And while structural changes in the industry have sometimes devastating repercussions at local and regional levels, these developments are often deemed necessary at central government level. Thus, inter-governmental relationships often tend to work against the interests of the city.

It is true – at least in a historical perspective – that national governments have come to the rescue of cities hit by massive job losses. Overall, however, the pattern remains that cities lack the key political instruments to control very much of the economic foundation of their existence. Here lies a fundamental political and democratic problem; what are the normative and constitutional values of local self-government and autonomy worth when a private corporation single-handedly can significantly weaken the economic base of the city by relocating to another city, perhaps even another country?

As the discussion thus far shows, the role of institutions in urban governance is a somewhat contested issue. We mentioned earlier that urbanists have traditionally looked at institutions with scepticism at best (but see Clarke 1995, Lowndes 2008, Sellers 2001) or simply ignored them at worst. Urbanists from a neo-Marxist background tend to dismiss local institutions as subordinate to the capitalist economy at the local, national and global levels, hence there is very little variation to expect, let alone to explain. Other observers of urban politics emphasize the significance of coalitions to promote growth in the local economy between the political elite and corporate interests. Again, if coalitions and networks operating outside the due political process by and large shape urban politics, then there should be little to gain from an institutional analysis of urban political behaviour. While one could certainly discuss the validity of those two objections to institutional study, the present analysis draws on a wider definition of institution, to reiterate an earlier remark.

This book substantiates the utility of an institutional analysis of urban governance that compares different normative patterns of urban governance and not just their structural underpinnings. These different normative patterns or institutions leave an imprint on the structural framework of local politics. Thus, for example, cities that make the pursuit of economic growth their overarching goal will design political institutions that are most likely to promote that goal. Similarly, cities with a strong commitment to welfare politics will organize themselves accordingly. It is this dual, but inter-related, meaning which sets contemporary institutional analysis aside from the less appealing formal presentation of organizational structure. It is with this dual meaning of institution in mind that we can understand the institutional dimensions of urban governance.

Four models of urban governance

Different models of urban governance have emerged and, over time, become institutionalized in different political, economic and social contexts. In this book, we look more closely at four such different models of urban governance: managerial, corporatist, pro-growth and welfare governance. Each model displays a set of objectives and goals for the city as well as the key constituencies sustaining governance; the institutions created to pursue the governance objectives; strategies for managing contingencies *vis-à-vis* key local actors in the city's external environment; and also the city's strategies *vis-à-vis* regional and central government.

Before we introduce the four models some general comments are relevant. First, the models are analytical, idealized models of urban governance. They are intended to show how a particular overarching urban policy objective shapes urban governance. As we will discuss in the concluding chapter, we should expect most cities to display some features of several, if not all, of the models.

Second, the typology is primarily intended for intra-national comparison and less for cross-national analyses. National context (political, institutional, economic and cultural factors) still shapes much of urban politics. That means, for instance, that growth-oriented governance plays out quite differently in countries in Southern Europe than it does in the United States. Welfare-centred governance will mean different things in Norway than it means in Turkey, to give another example. Corporatist governance is clearly more relevant to some national contexts than others and so on. The point here is that the typology seeks to show how different values and norms in urban policy shape urban governance.

Third, it is not possible to design a typology of urban governance, or probably anything else for that matter, that fits perfectly with all the cities around the world. The analysis presented in the book is clearly more relevant for cities in developed countries, particularly the western world, than it is for cities in the Third World.

In managerial governance, which is the first of the four models, the emphasis is on relaxing political control over the city administration and service production. Public services are frequently contracted out or privatized. Service production is oriented more by 'customer' choice than by political decisions. Managers are given substantive discretion and autonomy, while elected officials mainly define long-term goals and objectives. Some readers may recognize this model of governance as a type of local politics alongside a New Public Management-style of administrative reform. The emphasis on managerialism and the downplaying of the role of politicians raises questions about democratic steering and accountability and also about transparency.

The second model of urban governance that we will be discussing is corporatist governance. This model highlights urban politics in the small, industrialized democracies in Western Europe and the role of organized interest in local government. While local corporatism allows local government to bring the 'third sector' into public service production and delivery, it also raises important questions about the 'governability' of the city.

The third model of urban governance is pro-growth governance, which is strongly influenced by the American debate on local economic development strategies and their impact on urban political choice. In 'pro-growth cities', economic growth becomes the overarching objective. This impairs distributive and redistributive urban policies since they – following Paul Peterson's often-cited model in *City Limits* – make the city less attractive for private business investment (Peterson 1981). The 'unitary interest' in economic growth – the notion that such growth is in everyone's interest and therefore above and beyond political debate – is discussed in detail. Also, the juxtaposition of market-conforming urban politics on the one hand, and political choice on the other, is discussed extensively.

The fourth and last urban governance model which will be discussed is welfare governance. It describes urban politics in declining industrial cities, which have become strongly dependent on financial support from the nation state. Stimulating economic growth becomes controversial; instead, there are strong sentiments for 'local socialism'. This model of urban governance is common in formerly prosperous industrial regions in Germany, the United States, the Scandinavian countries and the UK.

The four governance models will be elaborated in subsequent chapters. This analysis will help us explain why different models of urban governance seem to evolve in different political and economic settings. This is not to suggest that those settings mechanically determine the form and objectives of urban governance. Rather, the book pursues the argument that urban policy choices can be critical in shaping the future of the city, whether it refers to political and economic priorities, strategy of economic development or urban public spending on culture. We know from a number of studies that cities do make such choices at critical junctures of their development and that those choices indeed matter (see, for example, Hall 1988; Jones and Bachelor 1986, Magnusson 1996, Pagano and Bowman 1995, Stone and Sanders 1987). Thus, the present analysis shares the belief with the group of urbanists who argue that local policy choice does indeed shape the urban future although such choice is to some extent a reflection of – and embedded in – the local society, that is, the configuration of the local business community, the significance of organized interests, as well as central local institutional relationships.

Chapter 3

The Managerial City

The managerial city is shorthand for urban governance dominated by non-elected officials, particularly senior-level administrators and managers. The managerial city has its intellectual roots in the perennial debate about the relationship between politicians and bureaucrats and also in the pervasive model of administrative reform in a large number of countries since the 1980s known as the New Public Management (NPM). Among UK cities, Birmingham might be a good example of a city where managers and a managerial philosophy shape urban governance. Managerial governance is probably more common in America than in Europe; indeed, a large number of cities and towns in the United States display urban governance where the city manager plays a leading role (Moore 1995). During the past couple of decades the notion of the professional city manager has become a role model for city governance and public management in the US. Since political and managerial leadership are to some extent communicating vessels, in order to understand managerial governance we must also look at the kind of political leadership which this models stipulates. Different models of city political leadership give professional managers different roles in the governing of the city.

In the managerial city, politicians define the long-term political and economic objectives, leaving managers extensive discretion in the implementation or 'operations' more broadly. This may produce smart and effective government – but it may also produce a city effectively governed by managers (see Rhodes and Wanna 2007). This chapter will discuss the blessings and perils of managerial governance of the city.

Politicians and managers: an uneasy relationship

Politicians and bureaucrats live in 'uneasy partnership', argue Joel Aberbach *et al.* in their seminal work on politico-administrative relationships, *Bureaucrats and Politicians in Western Democracies* (Aberbach *et al.* 1981). While there is much to suggest that that is the case at the central government level, we will argue in this chapter that, everything else being equal, politico-administrative relationships in local government are more characterized by symbiosis and partnership than those relationships are at the central government level. There are several political and institutional reasons for this difference between the different tiers of government, which will be discussed later in this chapter.

One element of the potentially strained relationship between politicians and bureaucrats is related to the different roles performed by politicians and managers. Politicians are (or are at least assumed to be) generalists, whereas bureaucrats are more specialized. This specialization is to some extent a function of the size of the bureaucracy and, arguably, of the size of the polity. Thus, in small local authorities managers are as likely to be generalists as are the elected politicians. Furthermore, in central government directives to bureaucrats frequently change as a result of political division. Local politics, on the other hand, tends to deal with less divisive issues, partly because of the smaller (and therefore more homogeneous) polity and partly because in most countries ideological issues are resolved primarily at the nation-state level and less so at the local level. For these reasons, we would expect local politics to be more pragmatic and consensual than national politics and we would also expect politicians and managers to have a less adversarial relationship at the local level compared to central government.

Another important difference between national and local politics is that the former tends to be more professionalized than the latter. Local politics in many countries still cherishes the notion of the layman politician; a *pro bono* political representative embedded in her community and not a part of the political machinery. And there was a time when local politics took pride in displaying less political division and conflict compared to national politics. For the most part, however, party line is a salient feature of local political decision-making. Furthermore, contemporary local politics, not least in Europe, is to a large extent shaped by ideological differences among the political parties.

All of this would suggest that city managers, being more continuously involved in city affairs than the politicians, develop more expertise and, as a result, more influence. To some extent, the office of city manager has historically – not least in the United States – been surrounded by the same romantic mystique as the local elective office. In this view, the city manager was the main caretaker of the town, operating above and beyond city politics and loyal to the city leaders of the day. However, this de Tocquevillian image of managerial governance might be an idealized image of the relationship between city politicians and bureaucrats, which says rather little about the current state of affairs.

It seems clear that the role of city managers underwent significant changes during the twentieth century. In an analysis of the changing role of city managers in American cities, Nalbandian and Portillo argue that city managers have gradually become more professionalized and are increasingly working in partnership with elected officials (Nalbandian and Portillo 2006). This development has been propelled in large part by the increasing scope of the city's service delivery and the sheer size of the city administration. While that appears plausible, the changing role of the city managers during the 1990s and early 2000s is also explained by the rapid emergence of NPM as a model of administrative reform. We will return to that issue later in this chapter. For now, the important point we wish to make is that there are several institutional and political factors which tend to accord the city managers – and the city administrative apparatus as a whole – an important, if not predominant, role in the city.

We mentioned in the previous chapter the two fundamental and potentially conflicting roles of the local authority

(Keating 1991). One role is derived from the democratic, participatory objective of urban governance, which portrays local government as a democratic arena and an instrument for the accommodation of political conflict. The other dimension is the managerial aspect, which sees local government as a public organization resolving collective needs and interests through service production and delivery. These two different aspects of local government place different – some might say even inconsistent – demands on local authorities. As a result of this tension, there has in many countries evolved a cycle, almost like a pendulum movement, with regard to which of the two aspects should be given priority in institutional reform. In some instances it can be difficult to ascertain to what extent local government reorganization – either conducted by the nation state or in a more spontaneous fashion by the local authority itself – serves managerial or democratic-participatory objectives.

Also, while the intention of a policy may be to enhance one of the aspects, it may very well end up strengthening the other aspect. For instance, in Sweden during the 1970s and 1980s, a comprehensive programme of local government amalgamation was conducted to create local governments that could assume greater welfare state responsibilities, that is, an emphasis on the managerial dimension of local authorities. While critics saw the drastically reduced number of elected offices as a threat to local democracy, the long-term effect of the reform appears to have been a stronger local democracy as well as a strengthening of the administrative and organizational capabilities of local authorities (see Strömberg and Westerståhl 1984). Similar reforms of municipal mergers are now discussed or implemented both in some of the Scandinavian countries and in Japan. Such mergers have become viewed as necessary as a result of increasing problems in maintaining high public-service levels in a time of a decreasing tax base and an increasing number of elderly in many small, rural municipalities. Again, this reform has not paid very much attention to the potential democratic downsides of such reform.

From the late 1990s through the 2000s, the managerial dimension has clearly come to dominate over the democratic-participatory dimension of local government. The main driver of this shift has been the exacerbated fiscal crisis of the state and local government (Sharpe 1988). The financial crisis has been coupled with a widespread orientation in most countries away from collective political involvement towards the pursuit of individual interests (Dalton 1996). Another important driver has been the rapid diffusion of the New Public Management model of public-service delivery (see below). This model emerged at the central government level but its concrete manifestation has been seen, not least at the local level.

The professionalization of local administration poses important problems for the pursuit of core local government policies such as economic development. Social workers frequently not only ignore the politics of growth; they also actively oppose it. To them, many of the problems they deal with in their daily work are manifestations of the downsides of pro-growth policies which do not cater to all segments of society. We can see similar patterns with regard to the other models of urban governance discussed in this book. The administrative elite of the local authority will also oppose corporatist governance, according a key role for organized urban interests in the local policy process – except, of course, when those interests coincide with those of the administrators. Welfare governance is likely to find support among social workers but less so among other groups of employees in the city administration. The key common denominator is that professionalization stands at odds with political control. Professionalization revolves around the idea that professional groups within the urban bureaucracy – teachers, social workers, managers, engineers, and so on – have advanced skills and training which should be allowed to shape their daily work. In this view, politicians – as generalists without detailed skills in these professions – should not interfere with the professionals' ideas abut good public services but instead only define the long-term objectives of their work (Laffin 1986, Nalbandian 1991). City managers, too, are weary of too much political control but they operate closer to the political leadership than most other administrators and are supposed to take the broader view on urban policy matters.

Urban managerialism

As a model of urban governance, the managerial city is sustained by a set of norms and beliefs about good urban governance. These norms are related to the traditional notion of the city manager as the city's caretaker. In addition, urban managerialism is sustained by norms espousing clean and effective government, a strong economic development and not wasting the taxpayers' money. Finally, it is a model of urban governance that acknowledges professionalism in urban service production and management. Together, these norms offer powerful support for urban managerialism and make it difficult for critics to find good arguments to attack the managerial objectives. The only conceivable opposition to this type of managerialism would be that it potentially challenges democracy in the city, but since managers have more or less been given their position by elected officials and report to them, even that argument is weak and far-fetched.

These traditional values and beliefs about the role of the city manager have, in the early years of the twenty-first century, been supplemented by another set of ideals related to public management, commonly known as the New Public Management. While NPM values in many ways correlate with the traditional norms in terms of emphasizing professionalism and 'good government', they also stress managerial autonomy as a means of creating a pure managerial role with a minimum of political or other interference. There are, however, also several important differences between the traditional and modern, NPM, managerial roles. In the traditional model, the city manager was first and foremost a public servant with all that entails in terms of upholding equal treatment, equality and impartiality. The NPM manager, by contrast, should preferably have a long background in the corporate sector so that s/he can manage public-service production in the same efficient manner as it is conducted in the private sector.

Urban managerialism focuses on getting the job done as quickly and cheaply as possible. The overarching objective of this model of governance is to build a service-producing organization which provides best possible services to the citizens of the city. City managers, of course, acknowledge that they are working in a political environment and that local government is not just about producing service but also catering to wider democratic objectives and functions. That having been said, however, managerial governance echoes de Tocqueville's image of the local populace as more homogeneous, and therefore less prone to political conflict, compared to the national *demos*. Just as is the case with pro-growth urban governance, managerial governance rests on an assumption about some degree of consensus for the chief objectives of this model of governance. If issues on the urban political agenda are politicized, that is, when there is a clear division between the political parties, there tends to be less manoeuvring space for the manager. However, it is inherently difficult to argue against effective urban management, just as it is (seemingly) difficult to argue against growth in the local economy. Who would not want effective and cheap urban service production and administration? And, if attaining those goals means giving the city manager more autonomy and control, then so be it. In fact, the urban political leadership tends to welcome the NPM model of division of labour because it means that they will not have to deal with the nitty-gritty details of routine decision-making and can concentrate on broader and more long-term policies.

City managers typically resolve the tension between their autonomy on the one hand and the need to ensure political approval on the other by routinely reporting back to the mayor's office or seeking *ex ante* approval on bigger issues and decisions. In large cities, where the city's political leadership are full-time employees, the risk of excessive managerial autonomy can be handled. In smaller towns, however, the city manager spends more time in city hall than the political leaders and that may jeopardize political control and accountability.

Objectives

This normative foundation, providing fertile soil for a wide variety of market-based concepts, is part and parcel of the NPM reform agenda which has found its way into local authorities across the western world and beyond (Pollitt 1990). NPM first emerged around 1990 in the debate on administrative reform at the central government level and set in train an unprecedented wave of public-sector reform in most countries of the world. Indeed, while there are indications that the NPM reform movement lost some momentum at the nation-state level, it has become a more permanent feature of urban (and in some cases regional) administrative modernization in several countries (Osborne 1988).

Essentially, NPM, as a model of administrative reform, denies any specificity of the public sector as a service producer; that is to say, public-service producers should be perceived as any other service-producing system. The main root and cause of inefficiencies in the public service, NPM advocates insist, is the existence of public monopolies and too much political control over what is being produced. The solution to these problems is to open up the public sector for market-based service producers. NPM emphasizes the need for competition among different service providers and the 'empowerment' of 'customers' (Osborne and Gaebler 1992). The overarching goal is to create a public choice-style, market-like exchange between the producers and consumers of urban services, where consumer choice rather than political preferences among elected officials decides what services will be offered.

The long-term objective of NPM is to create a public service which delivers better and customer-attuned services, which cost less and ensure customer satisfaction. By opening up the public-sector service production for competition from the private sector, privatizing and contracting out services and by

facilitating customer choice among different service producers, this is a model of administrative reform which seeks to
produce a modern system of service production.

NPM has a generic view on management (Peters 2001: 28,
see also Moore 1995); since, according to this model, there
does not exist any significant difference between public- and
private-sector service production, managing organizations in
both sectors is basically the same kind of challenge. In the
NPM reform campaign, it is essential that politicians should
only define the long-term goals and objectives of the public
service and then 'let the managers manage' (Osborne and
Gaebler 1992). This aspect of NPM is particularly important
in an analysis of urban managerialism, as it helps us understand why elected officials so willingly surrender much of their
former control over the public service. NPM-style managers
are experts in leading large-scale organizations, and their
mission in the public sector is to reduce costs and deliver
services which the 'customers' demand.

Thus, in addition to the normative base of urban managerialism mentioned earlier – clean and honest government, economic growth and a sound management of the city's financial
resources – we should also add the legitimacy that comes with
bringing in private-sector management experts into the public service. The public sector has, for a very long time, been
accused of inefficiency and lack of professionalism. By bringing in managerial experience from the competitive market,
this critique is to some extent silenced.

Instruments

Given the wide and encompassing objectives of the NPM
agenda, this type of administrative reform draws on a large
number of instruments. Equally important, however, NPM not
only seeks to adjust the existing public-service system, but also
to change the fundamental structure and modus operandi of
the system. Such profound transformations are not possible
unless the normative underpinnings of the institutional system

are changed as well. Thus, one of the most important – but frequently overlooked – instruments of the managerial city is based on a critique of the urban politics discourse. At the level of the nation state, NPM was prefaced by an assault on the traditional model of public-service delivery. The public sector was portrayed as inefficient, expensive and not responsive to clients' needs; civil servants were said to be privileged (Hood 1995, Savoie 1994); and citizens were described as a collective of powerless taxpayers, providing the financial means for a public sector which did not care too much about delivery, let alone 'customer satisfaction'.

Cities, too, were exposed to that critique. In some ways, since the overwhelming majority of exchanges between citizens and the public sector occur at the local level, local providers of public services have often been the primary targets for frustration over public-service quality or inertia.

The main instruments of managerial governance relate to the institutional role of the urban managers – by which we refer not only to the city manager but to the senior administrative echelon of the local authority – and the forms of exchange between the city and the market which this model of urban governance displays. Thus, one important instrument has been a gradual shift in power and control from elective office to professional managers. The general philosophy has been to give managers more autonomy in their managing role. At the same time, the key role of elected officials was redefined to formulate the long-term goals and objectives of service delivery.

This strengthened role of the city manager fits well with the development in American cities towards a partnership rather than a hierarchy between the city manager and the senior elected officials. It is also in line with the long-established model in the Scandinavian countries to have cities employ senior politicians in order to give them an opportunity to match the expertise of city bureaucrats. In both of these national contexts, the top administrative manager in the city operates in fairly close contact with politicians but at the same time enjoys fairly extensive autonomy. Consultations between the top political and administrative leadership have become less hierarchical, more informal and more reflective of a partnership than of a principal–agent relationship.

A second set of instruments is related to the involvement of the private sector in service production and delivery. The enhanced autonomy of the city's administrative leadership is, in turn, a prerequisite for its closer relationship with the private sector. In this model of urban governance, there is a strong belief that the private sector is superior to the public sector in terms of producing high-quality services at a low cost. Therefore, service production should be acquired on a competitive basis to the largest extent possible. By 'contracting out', the city manages service production through contracts with public-sector companies. Services are still tax-financed but are provided by the private company – or organizations within the city administration – that put in the best tender. Thus, the city administration ensures that services decided at the political level are provided at the lowest possible cost. It is not itself involved in the production of those services, but, from the point of view of the recipients of the services, the important thing is that they are provided. This is 'steering, not rowing', as Osborne and Gaebler (1992) put it; the city does what it should do while leaving service production to those who do it best.

Moreover, management by contract is often institutionalized in so-called purchaser-provider models. Here, politicians play the role of purchasers whereas providers can be private-sector organizations, civil society or service-producing departments within the city administration, operating in a competitive market for contracts. The important aspect to notice about the model is that it seeks to clarify roles; politicians should not be involved in the 'operative stages' of the service-delivery process, and producers should not interfere with decisions regarding which services to purchase.

Contracting out and purchaser-provider models are today common features in the urban political milieu around the world. While there are many positive aspects of such managerial inventions in public-service provision, we should also be aware that they are not without deficiencies. Managing by contract is a process which requires sizeable staff and resources, including legal expertise, in the city administration. Competitive tenders only work if the purchaser has the capability to define what is to be purchased, which criteria should be used to evaluate the bids and how to monitor and evaluate the services provided. Thus, there are not only gains to be calculated from the model but costs as well. Furthermore, despite almost any degree of fine-print control in the contracts, it seems as if issues of accountability surface as soon as there is evidence of poor quality of the services delivered (Thomas 1998).

A final instrument of managerial governance is internal markets. Departments within the administration buy and sell services from each other, instead of simply offering them for free. That way, costs are charged to purchasers, resource allocation becomes more visible and accurate, and accountability clearer. Internal markets were first used in the medical-care sector but have since then become a rather widespread concept. However, if the old model could be accused of leading to excessive demand, internal markets easily lead to excessive supply. This becomes particularly clear in sectors where there is a great deal of professional judgement involved in decisions concerning which services should be offered. Again, in the medical sector, patients from outside jurisdictions tend to be 'offered' procedures, which might not be entirely necessary, since the costs can be charged to the patient's home jurisdiction. Thus, internal markets may lead to over-consumption of public goods since they create incentives for excessive services when the cost is charged to another authority.

There are other instruments in managerial governance but the ones discussed here seem to be the most important and also most common. Thus, the key instruments in managerial governance are not so much the kind of specific policy instruments or policy measures we usually think of when we discuss instruments. Instead, managerial governance builds on a more overarching change in the centre of gravity in the city leadership. Elective officials are expected to define long-term goals and leave managers sufficient autonomy to enable them to reach those goals.

Outcomes

Managerial governance, as we have seen, has many virtues and its outcomes should be quite palatable to the local public. NPM provides customer choice in public service, cuts costs, measures customer satisfaction, allows politicians to focus on long-term policy objectives and facilitates a tight budgetary control. Furthermore, by placing management and not politics in the driver's seat there are also better possibilities for policies which draw on concepts such as 'model cities' or 'best practice'. Since managers, not politicians, make the day-to-day decisions regarding service production, distortions from the political debate never reach the manager's desk. Instead, s/he can engage in the community of other senior urban managers, thus diffusing ideas and concepts of good public service.

Managerial governance is also financially conservative. While we see few examples of urban managerialism where taxes have been raised to expand public services, there are a fair number of cases where that managerialism has spurred local politicians to cut taxes and public expenditure. Since managerialism revolves around the question of how to produce better services at a lower cost, there is nothing inherent in NPM, which does not make it a useful instrument in a political context characterized by an expanding domain of public services. However, the discourse of managerial governance, with its emphasis on market ideals and small government, effectively makes NPM not only a useful strategy to increase efficiency but also a powerful tool to promote a shrinking city budget. Contemporary city managers are professional, well-trained and highly competent leaders of the urban bureaucracy, frequently with a background in the private sector, and there has been a widespread ideal to run cities much in the same ways as companies.

This philosophy indicates a rejection of a politically controlled urban bureaucracy, at least as far as its service production is concerned. It also suggests a rejection of a specificity of the urban service production (Pierre 2000); one of the myths about the public sector, according to the NPM advocates, is that it differs in significant aspects from private-sector organizations. By giving city managers extensive control over the 'operative' stages of the policy process and also the autonomy necessary for them to play that role, much of that specificity – to the extent that it exists – has been removed. This autonomy is thus both a prerequisite for efficient public management and also a means of protecting the city managers from political steering. We mentioned earlier in this chapter the dual role of urban institutions; on the one hand to be a democratic arena and an institution which enables citizens to have an input on how their city is governed, and on the other hand an institutional system to produce public services. In managerial governance, the latter function has clearly taken precedence over the former.

Managerial governance in perspective

Does managerial governance represent a shift in power in the city from the de Tocquevillian ideal of the small town governed by a responsive elected leadership and a city manager looking to serve the citizens? Have the managers 'taken over'? Well, yes and no. Yes, insofar as concerns the daily management of the city's service production and also to some extent in terms of organizational control. But all major, strategic decisions still rest with the politicians and the increased managerial autonomy could be seen as a model of division of labour where political and administrative roles have been made clearer and more distinct. Also, at the end of the day the accountability for public services still rests with the elected officials, an arrangement which sets up fairly strong incentives for politicians to keep some control over the city's administrative organizations. You rarely hear city politicians complaining about a loss of power to the managers; it is more common to hear them praising the system because it gives them more time to concentrate on more long-term issues. The daily management of a town, let alone a larger city, is a task of such magnitude that it requires a professional staff. It appears as if we have come a long way from the days when a small group of elected leaders and a dedicated city manager could handle the business of running a town or municipality. The popularity of managerial governance is proof of the need for specialization in urban management, and the need for skilled staff and administrative autonomy.

All of this having been said, however, managerial governance in its more extreme forms may be problematic for the democratic nature of local government. One problem is similar to the line-staff problem in organization theory wherein the staff, due to its closeness to and continuous interaction with the organization's leadership, acquires more influence than the line departments in the organization. It can be difficult for a mayor to argue against the city manager on issues where the manager has much better knowledge and knows what happens when the rubber meets the road. And the manager, therefore, easily become more influential on urban policy matters than his position in the city apparatus would suggest.

More broadly, there are tensions between an urban policy style, which gives priority to citizens' involvement and input on local public affairs on the one hand, and managerial governance on the other. Managers could easily argue against citizens' proposals if they do not fit the strategic plan of the city, or threaten to undermine the city's budgetary balance. The discourse of managerial governance puts economy over politics, hence there will be resistance towards proposals which would put political choice over economic calculi. Elected politicians tend to find this debate somewhat difficult to handle. On the one hand, they applaud managerial governance for its focus on the economy and inexpensive service delivery. On the other hand, they are to take a broader democratic responsibility for the city, which means not just managing the local economy but promoting democratic values as well.

As we critically examine urban managerialism we should focus on two issues. First, what kind of challenge has NPM posed to the local authority? The local authority suffers from much of the same institutional inertia and fragmentation as the nation state. To a large degree, this inertia stems from the fact that the urban political and administrative institutions are arguably more deeply embedded in systems of social norms, values and meaning than national institutions. As citizens of the city, we have rather firm and clear expectations regarding its functions and roles, and we appreciate the proximity and accessibility of local institutions. These expectations are to large degree manifestations of political culture, but also of the historical performance of the local authority. In Scandinavian countries parents with small children expect the city to provide cheap and high-quality public day care. In the United States, city officials would be confused and concerned if a parent called the city service and asked about public day care for her child. These institutionalized patterns of expectations on the city's services become manifested in the institutional design of the city. To what extent has the local administration proven capable of adapting to NPM as a new philosophy of city management and service production, and to what extent have citizens and clients adapted to that new philosophy? These are issues which will probably become more salient and be debated further.

Second, we need to assess how this revolution in public management has affected urban governance. It is clear that NPM entails significant reshuffling of the roles of elected politicians, city managers and city employees at all levels, as well as citizens, or clients, or customers, depending on which vernacular is preferred. Managerial governance suggests that the source of legitimacy for the public sector is changing. In the traditional, 'hierarchical' model of governance, legitimacy was primarily derived from the core values that guided public-administrative behaviour: due process, procedural justice, equal treatment, equity, transparency and accountability. Managerialism does not necessarily reject those values but it questions their significance. '*People don't want standardized services any more*', say Osborne and Gaebler (1992: 183, italics in original); people today are selective customers and want the city to deliver services which are tailored to their specific needs. The services that the city delivers – and therefore city politics as a whole – are legitimate as long as it delivers high-quality, low-cost tailored services. Thus, with some exaggeration, we could say that in the traditional system process was more important than outcomes, whereas in the contemporary system outcome justifies process.

NPM and the city

E. E. Schattschneider once wrote that 'there is a profound internal inconsistency in the idea of nonpartisan local self-government' (Schattschneider 1960: 9). To many observers, local government has a role in fostering democracy to its citizens, and political parties and political discourse are integral to local government (see Hill 1974). This does not preclude the idea that local government and local elected officials should first and foremost cater to the urban populace and issues that are politicized nationally need not necessarily find expression in the local political debate.

The managerial city tells us much about the significance of the institutions of the local authority. Urban governance in this model has defined organizational structures and roles which cater to managerial discretion and autonomy, with elected officials performing not very many other roles than a democratic linkage – and a fragile linkage it is – between the city and its dwellers. That democratic linkage consists primarily of accountability in terms of politicians' goal definition. Managerial accountability is still shaped by a relationship between politicians and civil servants, but is far more indirect and vague compared to the traditional model of city governance.

Unrestrained managerialism thus undercuts some of the institutional, normative and political integrity of the city. It is a model of urban governance which, following Stone (1989), enhances the capacity of the city to act, but it may also, at the same time, undermine its capacity to govern. Governing a city is more than a matter of cutting costs and keeping the customer satisfied; it is also about making complex and tough choices and to implement those choices. For the city to be able to do that, it needs some degree of insulation and protection from parochial interests and the market. By emphasizing cutbacks, a 'leaner and meaner' bureaucracy and a stronger reliance on the market, urban managerialism potentially challenges values inherent in the local bureaucracy which lie far above and beyond issues of efficient service production; values concerning collective action, distribution and redistribution and about the relationship between the citizen and the city.

At first glance, the managerial city has many attractive features. There is a clear definition of roles which allows different actors to do what they do best. There is a focus on resources and budgetary balance. There is a strong emphasis on professional administration. And there is a focus on serving the customers of the public services, taxpayers.

The potential downsides of managerial governance are much less obvious and tangible. They relate not so much to service production and delivery but more to the impact of managerial governance on the city and the role of urban politics in local society. Ezra Suleiman, in a critical study on recent administrative reform in several countries, is quite sceptical regarding the idea of looking at citizens as customers. Customers, he argues, 'are not a collectivity' (Suleiman 2003: 55). By bringing customer choice into the public service sector and at the same time downplaying the role of politicians and policy choice in the city, citizens have much less incentive than previously to engage in public, political debate. By exercising their right to choose, they can influence public-service production directly, individually. Some find this an extremely attractive way of empowering the individual in his/her relation to public institutions. Others, like Suleiman, bemoan this development since it may lead to a disaggregation of the polity and a loss of political debate.

Furthermore, the focus on costs, demand and professional management, which is the centrepiece of the NPM strategy, clearly has a lot to offer to public-service producers at all levels of government. The rapid expansion of urban services has probably created some degree of organizational 'slack' in most countries. Also, in an era when tax levels and public expenditures are constantly questioned and when the support for politicians and their organizations is soaring, increasing cost-awareness and professionalization in service production is an important strategy to alleviate problems of public distrust and strained public finances.

That having been said, however, managerial governance also poses several major challenges for local authorities. First, NPM assumes that service producers operate at arms-length distance from elected officials, whose main role is confined to defining long-term objectives for the urban service production. Within these broadly defined parameters, service production is to be guided via direct, market-like communication between producers and 'customers'. Obviously, the marginalization of elected officials is a very different enterprise and has very different consequences in the United States and Western Europe owing to the different historical roles local politicians have played in these different political milieus. In Western Europe, urban politics has always had a stronger partisan element than in the United States, although ironically a larger number of public offices are elective in the US than in most Western European systems. A common problem, however, seems to be to define alternative models of accountability; while NPM advocates argue that managerial governance offers citizens/customers a more direct and influential input on urban public services compared to the traditional system of local government (Osborne and Gaebler 1992), they also tend to be conspicuously quiet on how their model defines political control and accountability. Should elected officials be held accountable for service production over which they have virtually no control?

Second, managerial governance pits local authorities in dependency on professional management resources inside and outside their organizations. Traditional qualities associated with public employment, such as education in public administration and law, do not carry much weight, as business management ideals are to govern public service production and delivery. To some extent this may well be a short-term problem. However, bringing in expertise from the private sector may be just as much a problem as a solution since these professional groups usually have problems understanding the public sector's obsession with due process and legality. The introduction of NPM thus means a clash of two distinctly different organizational and professional cultures which will not be easily resolved. Values that are indigenous to the public sector and public office are alien to strict business management thinking, and vice versa.

Finally, bringing NPM into urban politics assumes a degree of organizational flexibility in local government which often does not exist, or which at least should not be taken for granted. Customer choice introduces an element of considerable uncertainty to local governments; if, for instance, parents are provided a choice with regard to what school they should send their children to, local authorities cannot plan education spending in different areas with the same degree of accuracy as in the previous problem which was based on demographic data and demand was predictable to a very high degree. In order to cope with this uncertainty, public organizations must be flexible enough to be able to reallocate resources at fairly short notice to those service areas where demand is biggest. Little surprise, therefore, that alongside the NPM campaign there is a similar plea for more flexible government (Peters 2001: ch. 4).

In sum, managerial governance accords only a minimal role to elected officials in urban governance. The emphasis is on output performance as defined, assessed and measured – incidentally one of the NPM buzzwords – according to private management standards. Managerial governance blurs the public–private distinction, not least on an ideological level by portraying service producers and clients as actors in markets and by identifying market-based criteria rather than legality as the key criteria for evaluation.

Chapter 4

Corporatist Governance

Most observers of contemporary western societies would probably agree that a strong civil society with NGOs and voluntary associations are a defining feature of democratic governance. These organizations offer citizens opportunities for collective involvement, which is not aimed at political institutions, or at least not to the same extent as is the case with political parties. Instead, civil society allows individuals to become involved only in those issues that matter the most to them, such as environmental protection or human rights or equal opportunity. True, the ultimate target of those efforts often tends to be different political institutions, but the scope of these organizations goes beyond the political. The urban scene displays a plethora of such organizations, some of which have a fairly clear political agenda and others which pursue their interests through other channels.

Corporatist governance is essentially urban governance featuring a significant and continuous involvement of civil society organizations in urban politics and public service delivery at the local level. These organizations make significant contributions to urban governance by providing opportunities for political and social mobilization, as well as offering a structure for public-service delivery which suffers neither from public-sector rigidities nor the narrow focus on profit which shapes market-based actors' behaviour (Clarke 2001). Amsterdam could be an example of a city where organized interests and social movements play an important role in shaping urban policy preferences and decisions. In a different political and institutional context, Singapore is a city with strong corporatist traditions where the three major ethnic groups – Chinese, Malay and Indians – form a particular type of social organization (Gugler 2004b: 12, Salaff 2004). However, as we shall see, some manifestation of corporatist governance is present in many different cities in different parts of the world.

The corporatist model of urban governance in its most advanced form is typical of the small, industrial, advanced democracies of Western Europe. These are political systems historically characterized by a strong étatiste tradition, which – with some national variation – manifests itself in a large public sector, redistributive policies, comprehensive welfare state service provisions, a high degree of political involvement, proportional representation and strong voluntary associations. It is tempting to suggest that these features are somehow causally related. However, corporatism at different levels of government per se does not seem to be the main cause of the high level of government spending; instead, corporatism and a large public sector are both derived from a distinctly collectivist political culture (Elder *et al.* 1982, Katzenstein 1984, 1985, Olsen 1986). That having been said, however, this chapter will argue that corporatist governance to some extent leaves the city captive of organized interests and therefore tends to pursue policies and programmes which are more reflective of the preferences of those interests than those of the city as a whole. The good news, from the point of view of democratic governance, is that not all organized interests share the same political objectives and so the local authority can to some extent play one against the other.

Another defining characteristic of corporatist governance is that it occurs primarily in the distributive sectors of local government. While the emphasis is on safeguarding and promoting the interests of the organization's members, there is also a strong commitment to participatory democracy in a broader sense. Furthermore, organization breeds counter-organization (Coser 1956), a process which in turn sustains high levels of collective participation and involvement. If the business community in a city organizes itself in a local business association we should expect environment protection groups and neighbourhood preservation groups to follow suit in order to match the collective power of the business community.

Corporatist governance, like all models of urban governance, is context-specific. The fact that it is primarily found in the high-tax, high-spend welfare-state countries in Western Europe suggests that this model of governance is more likely to occur in political contexts when there exist substantial incentives to organize, that is to say, strong organizations aimed at influencing the state and its policies seem to evolve in political contexts where the state implements extensive distributive and redistributive policies and programmes. Again, however, one of the perennial questions related to corporatist governance is the chicken–egg question of whether such governance drives such programmes or whether, conversely, those programmes encourage the emergence of a strong civil society.

It is easy to take a critical stance towards corporatist governance, arguing that it entails inequality in terms of representation and produces uneven outcomes in terms of distributive programmes and policies. But this model of governance has a range of virtues and positive values that we associate with urban democratic governance. While critics might argue that it creates a politically charged society, not everyone agrees that this is necessarily a bad thing if politicization also means citizen involvement and a public discourse on matters of common concern. Also, we should note that what in some countries was noted as a 'new' aspect of governance in the 1990s, not least in the UK (Rhodes 1997, Stoker 1998), was the inclusion of civil society and organized interests more broadly into the process of public-service delivery. Thus, like all models of urban governance covered in this book, corporatist governance too is a mixed blessing with features that can be both conducive to, or obstruct, democratic urban governance. And, like all the other models of urban governance, it offers challenges as well as opportunities for the city.

Corporatist governance in its purest form is based on the more or less continuous presence of organized interests in the policy process. However, the problems (as well as the positive aspects) associated with this type of governance surface also in less conspicuous contexts of corporatist governance. In the Scandinavian countries, but also elsewhere, creating institutional channels for the users of public services has become a popular way of empowering the individual *vis-à-vis* the city.

This has raised a series of complex issues about how the influence of users should be balanced against that of local elected officials (Jarl 2005). If users of a public service have substantive influence on that service they will place elected officials in the awkward position of being responsible for something they do not control. If, on the other hand, users have very limited influence despite their being members of a users' board, they could easily get the impression that they are being co-opted in order to prevent criticism for poor quality of services and a disinterest in engaging the users of public services.

These issues are present also in the debate on stakeholderism, which suggests that those public-service recipients and those who are affected by a public authority should have a say on the policies and decisions made by that authority (see Ackerman and Alstott 1999). Stakeholderism emphasizes that those with an interest in a particular public service – a university, a day-care centre or a hospital – should have some form of institutionalized means of influencing that service. The problem with the model is that stakeholders will have multiple opportunities to influence public services, as stakeholders and as citizens or voters, which creates some degree of inequality.

Another approach to modernizing governance by bringing in social movements and associations was put forward by the late Paul Hirst. He saw corporatist governance in the form of associative democracy as an attractive alternative to the traditional model of democratic governance in an era of globalization and a 'hollowing out' of the state (Hirst 1994, 2000). Hirst argues that the model of democratic governance that existed in the early years of democracy is far less appropriate and efficient today and needs to be modernized and supplemented by a bigger role for associations. Thus, as soon as we open up the discussion on corporatist governance we find that it appears in many different forms and shapes around the world and is attractive to scholars of modern governance.

The image of the 'new governance' as a broad, encompassing process crossing the public–private border, as portrayed by Rod Rhodes and others, is rather quiet on the reciprocal nature of civil society's involvement in public-service provision. Organizations involved in the production of social services tend to have fairly clear ideas about what constitutes good services and they will therefore seek to influence decision-makers to design services according to their preferences. Thus, corporatist governance is essentially a two-way street where the leverage and organizational resources that organized interests make available to the city come at the price of allowing those organizations substantive input on city politics. Cities may collaborate with sports clubs to facilitate leisure-time activities for children and youngsters, or with other types of NGOs in areas such as assisting homeless people or people suffering from various types of handicaps or other groups of people in need of special assistance. This type of collaboration has sometimes become highly institutionalized. Indeed, NGOs involved in these collaborative projects sometimes have internal debates about whether these arrangements are altogether good for the organization, as they can mean losing a great deal of autonomy.

Another type of organization that should be mentioned in this context is professional organizations. These organizations mobilize employees with some particular form of education and profession – for instance, social workers, teachers or medical doctors. The main purpose of professional organizations is to promote the profession and to reproduce values and norms regarding professional conduct, broadly defined. This means that several groups of city employees are also members of a professional organization and take their professional cues from those organizations. For the most part, this dual signalling system does not pose a problem, since local authorities see little reason to interfere with professional norms. However, cutback politics tend to bring tensions between the local authority and professional organizations to the surface; these organizations tend to take a critical stance towards drastic cutbacks in areas such as social services and education, on the grounds that it undercuts the quality of those services and may have dire consequences for the clients. Also, since professional organizations operate primarily at a national level, they indirectly tend to issue national standards that impair reforms aiming at decentralization (Laffin 1986).

Again, professional organizations are not the kind of mass-membership associations we normally associate with corporatism, but it is clear that they exercise substantive influence on city politics. Moreover, this influence is exercised from within the public sector and is thus probably more difficult to deal with, compared to outside groups or constituencies. Ironically to some extent, professionals are hired precisely because they are professionals and their objectives to produce (in their opinion) good public service usually reflect the objectives of the political level of the city. Conflicts typically emerge when politicians want to redistribute resources or cut back on public expenditure or implement organizational changes that professional groups find detrimental to the production of good public services. The root of disagreements between politicians and professionals tends to be that professionals are primarily concerned with the content and quality of the service they deliver, whereas managers and politicians must weigh that quality against the costs.

In the United States, different forms of neighbourhood organizations constitute one of the main groups to have the urban political leadership as its main target (Ferman 1996, Jezierki 1990, Kotler 1969). There seems to be significant national and cross-national variations in terms of the influence these organizations can muster in local politics. Neighbourhood politics has a particularly long history in Pittsburgh and, even today, neighbourhoods there are cohesive, well organized and respected in city politics. Unlike most other organizations discussed here, however, neighbourhood organizations are typically single-purpose and, thus, highly selective about which issues they should become engaged in.

Another significant type of organization with a significant stake in city politics is local business organizations. This relationship is at the core of urban political economy and urban governance of economic development, which we will discuss in the next chapter. In the present context, we should note that local business organizations – for instance, Chambers of Commerce or trade associations – are important players in urban governance. Given the city's critical dependency on private capital as a source of jobs and economic growth that might appear to be a rather banal statement, but local business organizations play a number of roles in urban governance that matter not only to private business but also to the city. From the point of view of the local authority, local business organizations make the dialogue with the business sector less complicated, since they greatly reduce the number of contacts. Without business organizations, local officials may have to maintain relationships with a large number of private companies; a vital local business organization representing the local business community means that the city only needs to maintain a relationship with that organization. Indeed, a study conducted in Sweden showed that, in order to make urban governance more effective, cities actively promoted the creation of local business organizations in locales where such organizations do not exist (Pierre 1992a).

The common denominator in the relationship between these different organizations and the political leadership of the city is that organizations pursue the interests of a narrowly defined social constituency, while the elected officials have to take a broader view. At the same time, those organizations are intermediate structures between the city and the surrounding society and are, as such, important actors in urban governance. In the governance style that has become popular over the 1990s and 2000s, cities have been expected to engage civil society and NGOs in public-service delivery. That would suggest that there are strategies available to the local political leadership that enable them to interact with external organizations without becoming their captives.

With regard to the relationship between users and professional and corporate actors, one could argue that these are not mass-membership organizations and that therefore the predicted clash between elective democracy and corporatist political influence never occurs. However, the central problem that we will discuss in this chapter relates to the pros and cons of various forms of involvement in the governance process by organizations and non-elected actors on governance. From that perspective, the difference between traditional forms of corporatism and the type of corporatist governance we discuss here is one of degree rather than one of matter.

We will, thus, treat the concept of corporatist urban govern-ance in a fairly relaxed way in the present context. It does not have to refer to the full-scale, mature manifestations we see in selected countries in Western Europe. Rather, the key aspect which this chapter will explore is the consequences of some degree of non-elective, collective and organized interest on urban governance. This means that we will look at the role of local business associations, groups of users of public serv-ices and other forms of collective interests, to investigate the logic and ramifications of their involvement in urban politics and governance.

Governance by civil society

As we argue throughout this book, different models of urban governance are manifestations of, and embedded in, systems of overarching societal values concerning the role of the state in society and collective goals. Corporatist governance portrays the city as a political and democratic system for the inclusion of social groups and organized interests in the urban political process. The idea of participatory local democracy manifested in interest representation is central to this model of urban governance. Equally important, policy deliberation is seen as a bargaining process among these interests (Hernes and Selvik 1983, Villadsen 1986). The chief role of the local authority in this perspective is to serve as an institution and process which can accommodate conflict, create consensus and organize con-certed public–private action. The key criterion of assessment is to what extent the city and its governance reflect the ideals of a participatory local democracy or of powerful organized interests.

There is, however, a very real danger involved in corporatist governance. While, in its notion of including civil society and its organizations into the policy process and in the delivery of public services, the city greatly enhances its 'capacity to act'

(Stone 1989) and its capacity to address social problems, there is a price to be paid for this model of governance which is often forgotten; these organizations will, for the most part, want to have a say on the objectives of the city's policies, which could create a privileged position in the urban policy process with resulting injustices between different constituencies in terms of political representation. However, not all NGOs involved in different ways in public-service delivery want to be involved in the policy process, and, indeed, some organizations have had rather intense internal debates concerning the risk of loss of integrity and identity as a result of becoming somewhat of a subsidiary to the city administration.

Objectives

The defining features of corporatist governance relate more to the organization of the policy process and the cast of actors in that process than to specific objectives. The advocates of this model of governance argue that the inclusion of civil society into the process of policy-making in the city is in itself an important objective. That position might appear to be at odds with traditional liberal democratic theory, which emphasizes a clear border between the political system and its environment (see Hirst 2000). However, urban governance has, for an extended period of time – and, for the most part, rightly so – been portrayed as an inclusive process, although few observers have acknowledged that such inclusion works both ways. Thus, an important objective for NGOs and other societal organizations is to become conceived of as legitimate and responsible partners to the city in the urban governance process.

Furthermore, those organizations obviously seek to use their access to city hall to promote the interests of their constituencies. In many ways, corporatist urban governance is aimed at the distributive aspect of urban politics. Some organizations, not least in the European countries, have an agenda related to social welfare and seek to ensure that welfare programmes are not cut back. Other organizations – for instance, those defending the rights and interests of the physically disabled – safeguard the interests of their members by ensuring that city services and urban facilities are geared to the special needs of their members. When local government refers to its autonomy when it denies those organizations the benefits they request, organized interests have, on several occasions, sought to promote legislation which they then can use to confront local authorities. Environmental protection groups tend to promote expansion of public transport in the city, recycling systems and bicycle paths. The list could be made much longer, but the general picture should be clear. Organized interests become involved in the urban policy process first and foremost to protect and promote the interests of their members and to pursue their agenda, and this usually requires some degree of public resources and spending.

If these are the objectives of the interest organizations, what – if any – are the systemic objectives of corporatist governance? There are traditional, as well as more contemporary, systemic objectives associated with corporatist governance. Traditionally, the inclusion of civil society into the urban political process was believed to be conducive to legitimacy and support for the political system; by opening up the political process to a wider variety of actors and interests, there would be a higher degree of involvement in public decision-making and a greater tolerance and respect for urban policy. Organized interests include mass-membership organizations; organizations at the local level are often branches of national organizations. Thus, the democratic culture and *modus operandi* of countries with a long corporatist tradition has for a long time featured some degree of interest-group involvement in public affairs, largely because it is believed to be the appropriate way to link the political process to society. The flipside to this arrangement, from the point of view of the organizations, is that they can become political 'hostages', that is, since they participated in the decision-making process they have forfeited their right to oppose disadvantageous decisions.

Bringing civil society and NGOs into the process of public-service delivery has been believed to be a means for the city to save financial resources. The general idea in the New Public Management model of administrative reform is that political institutions should 'steer, not row' (Osborne and Gaebler 1992, Pollitt and Bouckaert 2004); the important thing is not whether it is the city, a private company, or an NGO that delivers a particular service, but rather that the service is properly produced and delivered. The city's main role, according to this philosophy, is not to deliver all services itself, but rather to coordinate the activities of a wide range of societal actors, including its own organization. This places urban governance at the juncture of managerial governance and corporatist governance.

Thus, unlike the other models of governance discussed in this book, the objectives of corporatist governance need to be assessed both at the systemic level and at the level of the organized interests. Corporatist governance is for the most part deeply rooted in the political culture and emphasizes collective action, both at the level of the polity and at the level of the individual organization. However, there is a negative correlation, a potential conflict, between the objectives of the individual organization and the polity. If corporatist governance allows organized interest to have a significant, if not decisive, input on urban policy, governance will appear to be successful from the point of view of the individual organization. At the same time, however, the city's policies will not reflect the preferences of all the citizens, only those of the organization's members. If, on the other hand, urban policy does not cater to the preferences of organized interests, policy will be more in tune with popular preferences but the local authority will leave civil society alienated. Thus, the key challenge – and an important governance objective in itself – in this model of governance is to give organized interests some degree of policy influence without, at the same time, allowing those interests to hijack the local authority and use urban policy for their own interests and constituencies. With some degree of simplification we could say that the city has an interest in maximizing the resources it can extract from civil society but, at the same time, minimizing the influence from those organizations on urban policy. Civil society has exactly the opposite objectives; maximizing influence and minimizing the amount of resources it makes available to the city. Thus, accommodation has to be reached through a process of negotiation and bargaining, see below.

Instruments

Given the extensive inter-organizational coordination that is a defining feature of corporatist urban governance, this model of urban governance requires that politicians have considerable organizational skills in handling formal and informal relationships with key players in the environment. Thus, from the point of view of the local authority, the problems and challenges in managing corporatist governance are not very different from those associated with New Public Management reform; how does a political institution exercise some form of control over an external organization over which it has no formal leverage? Equally important, what are the challenges involved in having such an institution become engaged through informal governance arrangements such as networks and partnerships?

The typical policy instruments used in this model of urban governance are 'soft', non-obtrusive instruments such as negotiations, bargaining and information. Also, financial instruments, primarily the transfer of public funds for NGOs' involvement in public service, are important, as well as management by contract. We should remember that what is here discussed as 'civil society' is, in the real world, usually a very heterogeneous set of organizations, and the city cannot treat them all alike. Thus, the gains generated by bringing in NGOs and other organizations into public-service delivery must be weighed against the costs of managing those contacts and the political input that these organizations will tend to request. An important instrument of corporatist governance is, therefore, building in-house capacity to organize and manage the exchanges with civil society. Also, having civil society engaged in public-service delivery exacerbates the fragmentation of the local authority since it brings different sections of the organization closer to its points of contact in the civil society.

In addition to these instruments, there must also be some degree of consensus concerning the meta-governance issues related to this model of urban governance; that is to say, there has to be some form of framework that regulates the access and influence of organized interests on the city's policies. As is the case in any governance model, power must not be divorced from responsibility and accountability, but that is a tricky issue in this particular model. Since organized interests cannot be held to political and democratic account, there have to be – normatively speaking – clear boundaries on the influence of these organizations. At the end of the day, only politicians are held to political account and they will have to be the ultimate judges of how much political clout civil society should be allowed.

Outcomes

Various forms of corporatist governance have been in effect for decades, if not longer, in a number of countries and cities. In countries like Switzerland and Austria, the notion of *Proporzdemokrati* ('proportional democracy') is used to describe the deeply rooted notion that democracy is exercised by and through mass-membership organizations. Similar arrangements have been in place for a long time in the Scandinavian countries and in the Netherlands, just to give a few examples. In the early years of the twenty-first century, however, a new version of corporatist governance has, under the heading of 'new governance' or 'urban governance', manifested itself in the UK. In this version, the perspective on civil society involvement is more instrumental than in those countries where this has been a pattern for an extended period of time. That said, the problems and outcomes of corporatist governance are quite similar; bringing NGOs, interest groups, local business associations, neighbourhood organizations and other elements of civil society into the process of public-service delivery has some clear outcomes and consequences regardless of the purpose and the novelty of this governance arrangement.

An important consequence of corporatist governance is that it blurs the distinction between special interests and the public interest. Organized interests provide the key channels of political communication between political organizations and the populace. In its most extreme form, corporatist governance is not so much a model where voluntary associations have successfully secured access to the political process but rather a type of urban governance in which local government is embedded in a society structured by organized interests at all levels of political representation, participation, deliberation and implementation. The main role of the local authority in this model of urban governance is to sustain the political process and to provide electoral input and control, but the exercise of political power is significantly circumscribed by civil society; indeed, so much so that it could be argued that the public interest is a reflection of the collectivity of special interests. This extreme form of corporatist governance gives citizens little choice but to join an organization if they want to have a say on urban public affairs.

This blurring of the boundary between the city's political institutions and its environment tends to leave observers in the Anglo-American democracies slightly more agitated than their colleagues in other parts of the world, where the organizational sphere of society is perceived not only as an asset to the city but as a prerequisite and a sign of healthy democratic governance. There is an element of naivety in the belief that civil society could be brought into urban governance and service delivery without wanting something in return for those services, financial compensation aside. Organizations are, first and foremost, instruments of interest articulation and the target of that articulation tends to be political institutions.

A more modest manifestation of corporatist governance would be where organized interests agree to assume responsibility for service delivery within their area – for instance, where sports clubs provide activities for teenagers, organizations for senior citizens provide activities for the elderly and so on, but where it is understood that the arrangement is strictly contractual and without any political consequence. This would essentially be the NPM, new governance version of corporatist governance. This could be an effective strategy to cut costs for the city, but, as we discussed earlier, it is not clear how sustainable this model will be in the longer term.

Corporatist governance in perspective

The corporatist model of urban governance takes on different manifestations in different national and cultural contexts. Countries that have a long tradition of corporatism at the national level – primarily the smaller industrialized democracies in Europe – also tend to be quite familiar with the inclusion of organized interests in policy processes at the local level. Conversely, to those countries that embraced the 'new governance' philosophy – mainly the Anglo-American democracies – the involvement of civil society in public service delivery was part of the novelty. The different historical trajectories of corporatist urban governance probably accounts for the different views which city leaders have on this model of governance.

At face value, there is something very appealing about corporatist governance. Politics is about collective action, and it only seems logical and appropriate that people who share a conviction or belief team up and form an organization, thus giving them an instrument to pursue their interests and helping them recruit more supporters. The problems associated with this model of governance become apparent when the pursuits of these organizations clash with the institutional role of elected officials and with the political parties. Democratic theory suggests that elected officials should cater to the polity as a whole, not only to their constituencies or to special-interest groups. In order to do so, political leaders will, from time to time, have to defend their position and fend off organized interests. Obviously, we can think of a very large number of organizations that do not have a political agenda. But many of the politically insignificant and passive groups tend to request financial support from time to time, or will want to voice their interests with a political official. For most organizations it is probably safe to say that they will, at some stage, engage political officials or institutions, and it is then that there will have to be some accommodation according to which the public interest has to be upheld in relationship to special or parochial interests.

Some form of corporatist governance is also at the heart of New Public Management and the 'new governance' theory, where the local authority is expected to 'steer, not row'. However, as anyone who has mastered a sailing boat in adverse weather conditions would know, steering can be almost as demanding as rowing. In order to steer effectively, the city's institutions must engage civil society and market organizations. Offers must be analysed, purchase contracts must be drafted and performance must be measured and evaluated. In the case of NGOs and organized interests there is also the political dimension of their inclusion to consider. All of this takes time and resources and requires a high degree of expertise of different kinds in the local authority.

Corporatist governance rests on a mutual dependence between the city and civil society. Both parties have strong incentives to engage the other, yet both parties also have a need to maintain some degree of integrity and insulation in that relationship. The local authority relies on the support of organized interests to deliver services in areas where it has limited points of contact and in-house competency, but it does not want to become the captive of those interests. To civil society, collaborating with the city is a strategy geared towards increasing resources and influence on city politics; however, organizations are also careful not to lose their identity and autonomy in the process. Needless to say, the more specific nature of the accommodation between the two parties varies significantly across countries and probably also between different cities.

Given the significance of distributive policies in corporatist governance, maintaining fiscal discipline often becomes a significant problem. In order to achieve compromises which are acceptable to all major represented interests, public spending frequently tends to exceed what is financially possible. While there is considerable interest among the voluntary associations in having an input on public expenditures, there are far fewer incentives to participate in discussions concerning urban revenues, except, of course, where the interests of the organizations are at stake. This form of 'collective self-interest' poses significant problems in urban governance because it tends to disaggregate the public interest and put local government in a weak bargaining position *vis-à-vis* interest organizations.

A second problem is that, arguably, corporatist urban governance is a fair-weather model of collective political choice. We stressed earlier the inclination of interest organizations to promote not just a collective interest but also participatory democracy as a form of governance. Defending such a form of governance is, of course, also in the self-interest of the organizations since it provides legitimacy for their political involvement. However, in times of extensive cutbacks in local government expenditures, the incentives for organized interests to participate decrease dramatically. The rationale of corporate involvement in urban governance remains, first and foremost, defending the interests of the organizations' various memberships; hence the target of the organizations' strategies will change as the economic viability of different tiers of government is altered. In Scandinavian countries, for instance, interest organizations for the disabled worked closely with local government for a large number of years. However, as local governments came under severe fiscal stress in the late 1980s, these organized interests reassessed their strategies and turned to the state to push for legislation defending the rights of the disabled *vis-à-vis* local authorities. Thus, one of the dilemmas in corporatist governance is that it renders the city dependent on actors who make no prejudgements about the virtues of local government and urban politics. Instead, they take an instrumental view on local authorities and their participation in urban governance is guided by such considerations.

Furthermore, a standard criticism that has been levied against all forms of corporatist involvement in governance is that it creates inequalities among citizens. Those who are members of organized interests enjoy multiple opportunities to influence policy, whereas those who are not members only have their vote on election day to use as an expression of their political preferences. This is a fair critique which the supporters of the models have not been able to dismiss. The common argument to counter this criticism is that a viable and dynamic civil society is a keystone of democratic governance. That may well be the case, but it does not resolve the problem of political inequality. This problem is present not only in the case of mass-membership organizations' influence on urban policy; it is equally significant when users' boards, to a larger or smaller extent, exert influence on a local school or a local hospital. Why should the parents of school children have more influence on the school's activities and resource spending than other taxpayers?

The key problem in corporatist governance is, thus, striking the balance between promoting a positive involvement of civil society and NGOs in the process of governing, on the one hand, and avoiding the local authority becoming a captive of organized interests, on the other. There is no universal formula for how that objective is attained. The political culture that fosters corporatist governance shapes both the self-image of organized interests and the institutions of the city, hence this is a model of urban governance which cannot be created or altered overnight. From the point of view of the local authority, civil society is an important ingredient in the process of governing but, as any cook will testify, too much of a good thing can spoil the meal.

Chapter 5

Pro-Growth Governance

Of the four governance models covered in this book, pro-growth governance is probably the easiest and least challenging to understand. The simplicity of the model is to some extent the genius of it; economic growth is something which everyone in the community benefits from, directly or indirectly, hence there is (or should be) very little opposition towards a governance arrangement to that purpose. At the same time, it is the governance model which has the biggest potential for entailing a loss of democracy in the city. That is because pro-growth governance tends to bring the political elite close to the downtown elite, an arrangement that jeopardizes transparency and accountability and raises political concerns for those constituencies that are not part of the pro-growth coalition. In other words: pro-growth governance could bring prosperity to the city and its dwellers but that growth would come at a price. But, again, economic development is something which everyone benefits from. Or do they? What could be the source of opposition towards pro-growth governance? What is it about this governance model that makes it so seemingly powerful? What is the evidence of the performance of this model, that is, what do we know about the pros and cons of urban pro-growth governance? These are the main issues we will explore in this chapter.

Many would probably think of Atlanta, Georgia, as the most obvious example of urban governance geared to economic growth, mainly because that is one of most studied cases of pro-growth governance in the context of 'urban regimes' (Stone 1989). In his seminal book on urban politics, Clarence Stone shows how the business elite in Atlanta forged a coalition, an 'urban regime', with the city's political leadership in order to boost economic development in the city. Both parties were necessary components in that project and both controlled resources that the other party needed. The downtown elite had the necessary financial resources and organizational capabilities while the political leaders could bring a swift handling of legal and administrative matters as well as political legitimacy to the table. The synergy that came out of the regime empowered the participants and significantly increased the 'capacity to act'. Changes in Atlanta's political leadership, notably the election of an African-American mayor, did not weaken the regime, although it meant that economic growth was supplemented with other policy objectives such as neighbourhood development. We will discuss the urban regime model in more detail later in this chapter.

Economic growth has for long been the undisputed policy goal for a very large number of cities, and the fact that not all have been as successful as Atlanta is no proof that they have been any less relentless in their pursuit of growth. Cities like Manchester, Marseille (Savitch and Kantor 2002), Pittsburgh (Ferman 1996) and Cleveland (Swanstrom 1985) are good examples of cities that have seen their economy decline, only to further emphasize the growth objective. Although disputed and challenged from time to time, growth and economic development never left the urban policy agenda. In Japan, during the 1950s and 1960s, the overall goal was to rapidly restore and modernize industry, and cities became the venues for this aggressive campaign. It took widespread health and environmental problems to force the political and administrative elite to pause, reflect and reassess the unilateral emphasis on growth (Steiner *et al.* 1980).

Urban governance geared to boost the local economy has been a leitmotif in urban political research for decades. Its peak occurred in the wake of massive economic restructuring in America and the United Kingdom during the 1980s and early 1990s. To some extent, scholars could lean on the broad political economy literature, which offers a more general understanding of the relationship between the political sphere of society and the economy. In the late 1970s, Charles Lindblom wrote about the 'privileged position of business'

(Lindblom 1977). His argument was that private capital becomes a leading political actor by virtue of its control over the sources of economic growth, something which is of critical interest to political institutions. Private business pays taxes (although local corporate taxes are not levied in all countries), support local markets and employ people who also, in turn, pay taxes and boost local demand. The increasing purchasing power in the local markets attracts new businesses to locate in the city. Once a city is embarked on that virtuous circle its economic future looks bright.

Thus, the private-business sector is of critical importance to the economy of the city. The actions – or non-actions (Offe 1984) – of the corporate sector can either help a city to prosper, or they can effectively seal the fate of a city. Townships like McKeesport and Duquesne in the river valleys in the greater Pittsburgh area were completely annihilated after the steel mills shut down in the 1980s, with the McDonald's restaurants one of the last businesses to leave. Many cities in Ohio and Indiana experienced similar crises. Europe, too, has extensive experience of the blow to the local economy that industrial restructuring entails. In the Ruhr valley in Germany, the British Midlands and northern Scandinavia, a large number of cities lost a major share of their populations as declining industries shut down, leaving their former employees with the choice of either relocating to find work, or, in some countries, staying on to live on social welfare. Sadly, the list of cities and regions that have suffered the full impact of economic restructuring could be made longer, but the point we wish to make should be clear. Private industry is the chief source of economic growth at the local level; at the same time, it potentially can deliver fatal blows to the local economy. Both of these circumstances con- stitute powerful incentives to the city leadership to engage the corporate sector in order to govern the city in ways which yield a strong, positive economic development.

Not surprisingly, corporate players, too, are well aware of the rules of the urban political economy and rarely hesitate to use them to their advantage. Given the city's depend- ency on private-business location and investment decisions, corporations in many countries, primarily the United States, have successfully played one city against another in order to secure tax incentives and other benefits from the city where they will invest. Thus, there has been a 'market inversion'; instead of companies competing among each other for attractive locations, cities are competing for corporate investment. Several observers have found this questionable, both from a normative point of view and from the point of tax-revenue spending (Kantor and Savitch 1993). Others, observing the same phenomena from a public-choice perspective, suggest that this market-like situation induces cities to cater to business interests and to provide better service, something that in the longer term is to the benefit of everyone. This is the essence of Paul Peterson's assumption about a unitary interest in growth that we discussed in Chapter 2 (Peterson 1981).

We must now ask ourselves what all this means in terms of urban governance. To get a better grip on that issue we need to elabourate somewhat on what political and economic forces bring local politicians apart, or, conversely, push them together. The relationship between city hall and private capital was probably never one of symmetry in terms of dependencies. In the mid-1980s, Jones and Bachelor noted that 'businessmen are becoming less and less interested in exercising direct influence over city politics. Politicians are becoming increasingly interested in influencing businessmen' (Jones and Bachelor 1986: 207). In a similar vein, Richard Child Hill, also in the mid-1980s, portrayed Detroit's bleak prospects in addressing its delicate dependency on the automobile industry thus:

> Detroit's fate has been wed to an economic base controlled by a small number of multinational corporations. Corporate stability and growth are premised upon the capacity to respond to changing national and international costs and conditions. The profit logic that once brought investment and growth to Detroit now brings disinvestment, decline and decay ... Private corporations accumulate and reinvest capital. Detroit does not. Capital is mobile; Detroit is not. (Hill 1984b: 321, 333)

Are these observations still valid? Is the 'plight' of an industrial city as portrayed by Hill and the delocalization of business – the detachment of business from place (Logan and Molotch 1987) – described by Jones and Bachelor only typical to an economy dominated by manufacturing industry, or is it, as neo-Marxist urban scholars would suggest, a defining structural feature of the subordinate position of political institutions *vis-à-vis* economic actors and interests (Castells 1973, Cockburn 1977)? The 1990s and 2000s have seen economic globalization emerge as a force of economic development and restructuring which would exacerbate the problem of delocalizing corporate actors. However, the important argument is not so much that many private businesses can relocate whenever and wherever that is deemed advantageous for profit-making, but rather that, however flexible businesses are, they will always have to be located somewhere and hence locales compete to develop the biggest comparative advantages for that specific location (Hirst and Thompson 1999). This scenario pits cities against each other, in competition for private investment, a pattern which, certainly for a long period of time, has been the case in most advanced capitalist democracies (Gurr and King 1987, Hernes and Selvik 1983, Peterson 1981).

If the delocalization argument is correct, Jones and Bachelor's observation would be as true in the early twenty-first century as it was in the 1980s and 1990s. Their analysis, interestingly, reflected the harsh reality of many industrial cities quite some time before we began to talk about globalization and the delocalization of large corporations. The reason, obviously, is that a large number of cities were quite familiar with the plight of having an economy which is pegged to corporate profit levels long before globalization and delocalization had entered the vernacular of academics and practitioners. To be sure, it is only a minor exaggeration to argue that globalization – the exposure of individual companies to global competition and the detachment of companies from their present locale – had been a defining feature of the political economy of most industrialized cities ever since industrialization began. And it is interesting to note how much urban political economy literature from the troubled 1980s still holds true, or indeed highlights problems in the urban political economy which have been exacerbated in the globalized economy. As we will argue in Chapter 8, exposure to the international economy is a contingency – as well as an opportunity – which many cities have lived with for several decades, if not centuries.

Delocalization is an essential matter in the context of pro-growth governance, or urban governance more broadly. If key societal actors lose attachment and commitment to the city where they are based they have very little reason to engage in the process of governance. If, on the other hand, corporations realize that the city and its services are important factors for the recruitment of skilled and specialized employees, they would be more inclined to engage with the city and to become involved in partnerships and other manifestations of organized governance.

The empirical evidence seems to suggest that there is a huge variation among different types of private businesses with regard to their willingness and capacity to relocate. Multinational corporations have always been able to locate their corporate headquarters where it has been deemed to be most advantageous. But for smaller businesses – which constitute the vast majority of private enterprise – relocating is not an option. Proximity to customers, to the local labour market and local networks of firms, an established position in the local market, skilled staff and a tradition in the city are among the many factors that prevent many small and medium-sized businesses, not least in the service sector, from seriously considering relocation. Summarizing a large research project on the significance of local production systems in a globalized economy, Patrick Le Galès and Carlo Trigilia argue that there is a 'growing territorial embedded-ness of manufacturing activities throughout Europe. There is not a decline but rather a rise of territorialization, despite the growth of globalizing trends in product and financial markets' (Le Galès and Trigilia 2004: 336). This 'growing territorial embeddedness', in turn, 'involves more dependence on [local collective consumption goods] ... these goods are increasingly produced through formalized mechanisms of governance, in which cooperation among public institutions and private actors is crucial, and in which a growing role is played by associative actors' (Le Galès and Trigilia 2004: 339). Thus, contrary to much of the globalization rhetoric, a variety of political, institutional and economic variables associated with place and locality still matter a great deal for private-sector actors. This finding offers support for the argument that delocalization remains the exception rather than the rule, and that local governance arrangements matter to corporate actors.

Equally important, Le Galès and Trigilia's finding that in this emerging local economy 'cooperation among public and private actors is crucial' speaks directly to issues of urban pro-growth governance. According to this pattern, globalization does not delocalize business, or at least not all businesses. Instead, it increases their 'territorial embeddedness' and strengthens the linkages between corporate and political actors. It would suggest that there might be some recognition of businesses' dependence on place and the political processes typical to their locale, something that perhaps would level the urban political-economy playing field.

How is this model of governance organized and institutionalized? Is there real policy choice involved in such governance? Some – although certainly not all – observers go so far as to suggest that the city's dependency on corporate players creates a 'unitary interest' (Peterson 1979, 1981) in growth, which is to say that the stake in growth becomes a policy objective above and beyond political debate: 'City politics is limited politics ... it is only a modest simplification to equate the interests of cities with the interests of their export industries' (Peterson 1981: 4, 23). In terms of urban governance, this means that private business becomes an extremely powerful voice in the local political process. The city becomes a 'growth machine' (Molotch 1976) with policies geared to respond to corporate interests and with economic growth as the undisputed policy goal.

Furthermore, in order to be effective and credible, growth politics has to be – and, according to Molotch (1976) nearly always is – supported by all major constituencies in the city because all constituencies benefit from growth, one way or the other. 'If we don't stand united we don't get United' was a slogan frequently used by one of the candidates in the 1992 mayoral election campaign in Indianapolis in the United States. The background was that United Airlines was at the time considering making a major investment in a maintenance facility at the Indianapolis airport, a project which had triggered local opposition from environmental protection groups. Such opposition, the other side in the campaign argued, was detrimental to the city's chances of getting United's investment, hence the slogan.

Most of the publications on urban political economy during the 1990s and 2000s have highlighted the capabilities of 'urban regimes' – informal 'pro-growth coalitions' between the political and corporate leadership in the city – to shape the urban politics agenda (see Elkin 1987, Mollenkopf 1983, Stoker 1995, Stone 1989). Such urban regimes, which can be seen as institutionalized forms of pro-growth governance, include not only 'growth coalitions' at the local level, but also the political culture and ideology of economic growth as the chief urban policy objective. Although urban regimes are shaped by the ways in which the city relates to its external environment, regime theory is almost devoid of the institutional foundation of pro-growth governance. Some cities, as we will see later in this chapter, elect not to make economic growth the main goal of their policies, a choice which obviously will influence the relationship between city hall and the downtown elite. In other cases, when economic development is a political top priority, forging alliances with the private-business sector becomes a natural strategic choice. These exchanges tend to become institutionalized over time and embedded in the social and political processes of governing the city.

Once the political and administrative institutions of the city are created, they foster and reproduce the culture, traditions, values and type of leadership they represent. As Montesqieu put it: 'At the birth of societies, the leaders of the republics create the institutions; thereafter, it is the institutions that form the leaders of republics' (quoted in Carrithers, 1986). Thus, once in place, the institutions of the city shape the objectives of the local leadership. Furthermore, those institutions not only respond to changes in its environment; they shape and 'enact' that environment (March and Olsen 1989). These aspects of the city are present in all the four models of urban governance discussed in this book, but they are particularly germane to the pro-growth model. This is because pro-growth governance signifies the strategic importance for the urban political leadership of creating governance arrangements with societal actors in order to be able to pursue core collective objectives. Corporatist governance, too, illustrates that element of urban governance, but only pro-growth governance displays coalitions with actors and interests that are critical to the pursuit of a political goal.

Stone (1989) suggests that the task of governing the urban economy is beyond the formal and effective powers of local authorities. This does not mean that public–private interaction exacerbates public actors' dependency on private involvement in urban governance. Rather, there is interdependence present in the public–private exchange process. Regardless of its leverage over economic processes or actors, local authorities control power bases which are critical to the business community and which can be traded by local authorities in return for loyalty to the region, early warning routines, involvement in joint projects, etc. As we mentioned earlier in this book, a study in Sweden showed that local business confronted local political institutions with demands, not only for traditional business assistance such as infrastructure or a speedy legal process on business-related matters, but also with demands covering the entire range of urban services such as medical care, day care for children, high-quality culture and leisure activities (Pierre 1992a, 1992b). The explanation for this pattern is that private businesses, in order to attract skilled expertise, need to be able to present a complete 'kit' which includes both good working conditions and also an overall high quality of life.

The important point we wish to make here is that these demands on public services substantiate the patterns of mutual dependencies between local political institutions and local businesses. Cities and businesses have a joint stake in competing for investment and attractive and skilled potential employees.

Interestingly, the growth of the service sector and the post-industrial economy has not made these local conditions any less important but apparently only more so. What is changing is the specific nature of those local conditions. For instance, local authorities in most countries today see broadband as integral to their economic development; indeed, Sonny Perdue, governor of Georgia in the US, refers to broadband as the 'new dial tone' (Neff 2007: 11). In a related vein, Peter Florida has delivered a forceful argument that the 'creative class' relocates to cities of diversity, openness and tolerance, hence cities have stakes in creating or maintaining such a culture (Florida 2002). From the point of view of local economic development, Florida's theory is problematic as the factors he identifies as crucial for regional economic growth are also the ones that are most difficult to manipulate by political institutions. Austin, Texas, can bask in the glow of being ranked most attractive US city for the 'creative class', but what specific measures should cities further down on the list take to improve their position? How do you change local cultures towards one of openness, creativity and tolerance?

Pro-growth governance and the governance of growth

We should be aware of the distinction between pro-growth governance on the one hand and the governance of growth on the other. Pro-growth governance, as defined in this book, is about the urban policies to promote economic growth and its exchanges with societal actors in that pursuit. The governance of growth, on the other hand, is a more complex issue about the organization of markets and the role of public institutions in promoting growth. While there is an overlap between the two aspects of economic governance, it is also important to be aware of the differences between them. In the present context, we look at the objectives, instruments and outcomes of pro-growth governance and also at the extent to which different cities give different priority to this economic growth as a policy objective.

Economic growth and policy choice

Pro-growth governance model is by far the most familiar abstraction of urban politics. Past decades have witnessed a sometimes fierce debate among social scientists, particularly in the United States, concerning our understanding of cities' stakes in growth and the nature of the urban political economy in a broader perspective (for reviews of this debate, see Gottdiener 1987, Hill 1984a, Kantor 1988, Swanstrom 1988, 1991, Vogel 1992). The main issue – or perhaps rather one of the main issues – has been to what extent the urban political economy allows for urban policy choice or whether cities perceive very little choice but to pursue policies which they believe are favourable to the business sector. Advocates of the 'politics matters' school of thought, while acknowledging the powerful influence of the capitalist economy both in structural terms and with regard to corporate decisions and strategies (concerning, e.g., location), maintain that all economic structural arrangements offer some degree of political choice (see, e.g., Jones and Bachelor 1986, Mollenkopf 1983, Parkinson and Judd 1988, Stone and Sanders 1987, Stone 1989, Swanstrom 1988, 1991). The trajectory of urban economic development reflects such choices made in the past (Pagano and Bowman 1995).

The issue about the existence and range of policy choice is important because 'to govern is to choose', to quote a familiar phrase; governance is to a large extent a matter of making choices. Such choices not only refer to policy choices but also include choice between different development strategies and choices regarding the configuration of network partners and the governance process in a broader perspective as well.

This juxtaposition of market determinism and political choice is unfortunate and misleading for a couple of reasons. First, it assumes that political choice, because such choices are made by political actors, by design produces interventionist policies and outcomes which differ from those which would have evolved in the absence of political choice. Harvey Molotch, seemingly responding to criticism for being overly structuralist in his seminal 'growth machine' theory (Molotch 1976), points out that pro-growth politics and political choice are by no means inconsistent features of an urban political economy: 'Cities pursued growth not because they had to, but because those who controlled their politics used them for this purpose' (Molotch 1990: 176). The incentives for such choice can be personal fortune-building, as Molotch indicates, but they can also be based on strictly political and ideological considerations and preferences.

Second, politics can 'matter' in a number of ways, of which policy choice is but one. According to Stone (1987: 5), political choice in urban economic development refers to 'the creation of a set of arrangements whereby accommodation is reached between the wielders of state power and the wielders of market power'. Thus, political factors in urban politics are not confined to choices regarding economic development strategy, which seems to be the tacit operationalization of 'political choice' in much of this literature. Politics can also 'matter' in a wide range of other aspects. One key decision that is overlooked in the US debate refers to whether the city should get seriously involved in economic development in the first place. In partisan local government systems such as those of the UK or Scandinavian countries, non-action is sometimes chosen for ideological reasons by both right-wing political elites, arguing that cities should not intervene in the market economy, and leftist political leaderships, on the grounds that close collaboration with private businesses would yield private capital a privileged position in urban politics (Parkinson 1990, Pierre 1992b).

For cities who decide to engage in local economic development – and this group includes the vast majority of cities in most jurisdictions – politics 'matters' in a number of ways, mainly related to economic development strategy. In the present context, our main interest is in political choice regarding the structuring of governance. Pro-growth governance is a model of urban governance which is characterized by close public–private interaction in the field of urban economic development. The preconditions for such cooperation, or what Savitch (1998) calls 'the ecology of public–private partnerships', are to a large extent related to overarching, national traditions of state strength and public presence in the markets. Local political choice regarding the organization of pro-growth governance can refer to the degree of inclusion or exclusion of different actors, or choice between different short-term and long-term objectives, or the nature of the city's relationship with higher levels of government (Gurr and King 1987, King 1987) or whether the city should embark on internationalization as a strategy to complement other strategies, just to give a few examples (see Chapter 8).

Thus, political choice in pro-growth governance has both an institutional dimension, in terms of the political, economic and cultural traditions pertaining to public organizations' presence in markets, and an organizational dimension, regarding the process of governance and what the role of public organizations should be in that process. These choices are embedded in the urban political economy but even so they remain, for the most part, genuine choices. They are choices not just about what the city should do, but also how it should do it, with whom it should do it and how this cooperation should be organized.

Urban political economy and pro-growth governance

Research on urban political economy was a leitmotif in urban politics during the 1980s and early 1990s. Since then, the urban political economy research agenda appears to have lost much of its attractiveness among urbanists. To some extent, similar research questions are now addressed under headings like 'regime politics' or 'global cities' or 'the internationalization of cities'.

Much of the debate on urban pro-growth governance has revolved around two issues. One issue has been the apparently hegemonic position of economic growth as a policy objective. We mentioned earlier Harvey Molotch's notion of 'the city as a growth machine' (Molotch 1976; see also Logan and Molotch 1987). Molotch's argument, in brief, is that pro-growth policies will encounter very little, if any, opposition because all major players have a stake in economic growth. Economic development strengthens the local labour market, increases demands on local services, increases the local tax base and makes the city a more interesting location for outside investment. Even if these developments primarily favour the urban middle class, the wealth generated by growth in the local economy will 'trickle down' – to use the phrase in vogue during the Reagan years in the United States – and eventually benefit also the lower classes in the city. Thus, one of the most important sources of strength in pro-growth governance is its ability to, seemingly, disarm all opposition by showing that this is the model of urban governance which everyone benefits from. The consequence of this apparent win–win situation is that concerns for urban congestion and environmental damage find it difficult to get on the urban policy agenda, let alone to have a significant constituency.

The other main issue in urban pro-growth governance, which flows directly out of the dominance of economic growth as a policy goal, is concerned with the purported 'privileged position' of business (Lindblom 1977). It is commonly understood that the chief engine in the local economy is not the public sector but private business; it is there that new jobs are created and commodities and services are produced. Therefore, catering to the needs and interests of local businesses becomes a political top priority, and local business organizations tend to find it easy to gain access to the urban political leadership (see Chapter 4).

Furthermore, the city's dependence on private businesses is said to foster an alliance between the urban political leadership and top corporate leaders involved in the aforementioned 'urban regime' (see Stone 1989). While forging such coalitions is a logical strategy for almost any city's leaders, the downside is that this close collaboration between private capital and the political leadership tends to side-step the due political process, shift urban policy towards business interests and, according to its critics, remove the actual decision-making from city hall to proverbial 'smoke-filled rooms', where the corporate and political elites strike deals and decide on the future of the city. Thus, the city's political leadership has to strike a delicate balance between engaging and assisting the business community without at the same time becoming its captive.

Together, these two features of urban pro-growth governance create a bias in urban politics, both in terms of the policy agenda and in terms of the relative political weight of different actors on the urban political scene. Some might argue that this pro-business bias in urban policy is the political price for the corporate sector's involvement in the local economy and in urban governance. Others point at the hazardous effects to local democracy of politicians becoming too cosy with business leaders. And, yet others – interestingly both conservative and more leftist-oriented observers – bemoan urban regimes on the grounds that politics and business should be kept separate and not interfere in each other's conduct (Pierre 1992b). Let us now look more closely at the objectives and instruments of pro-growth urban governance.

Objectives

Pro-growth governance is essentially the structuring of concerted, public–private actions to boost the local economy. Such collaboration rests on shared interests in economic growth between city hall and the downtown business elite. This model of urban governance is clearly the least participatory of the four models. Mass involvement could never be an option simply because such participation would immediately politicize the pro-growth strategy by bringing in alternative spending options, such as neighbourhood redevelopment and other distributive measures (Swanstrom 1985). While pro-growth politics has very few opponents – most local actors have a direct or indirect stake in growth (Molotch 1976, Logan and Molotch 1987) – it tends to have even fewer active supporters, apart, of course, from the public and private elites themselves.

Instruments

Needless to say, there is very little that the city can do itself to generate growth; this is something only private businesses can generate. Furthermore, the local economy is embedded in national and global economic systems over which the city has no control. Within those constraints, however, local government can make extremely important contributions to facilitating favourable preconditions for growth – for example, by using fiscal strategies which do not interfere with the growth process and by providing the necessary infrastructure and social services to attract business investment. Thus, the decisions and actions of public organizations become largely subordinate to the needs of private businesses, and the key criterion for the local government's decisions and actions becomes what they contribute to, how they remove obstacles to, private economic growth.

The instruments of pro-growth governance are, for the most part, indirect instruments that seek to facilitate growth and remove obstacles to growth. While all the major players on the urban political scene tend to subscribe to the policy goal of economic growth, some argue that there is very little the city (or any other political institution) can do to promote growth. Others maintain, from different normative strands, that urban politics should not engage the local business community, as that is essentially 'sleeping with the enemy', or, alternatively, that politics and markets should be kept separate because politics should not seek to interfere in the economy (Pierre 1992a, 1992b).

Since one of the purposes of the current exercise is to develop a taxonomy of urban governance which may serve as an analytical tool in intra-national and possibly also cross comparative research, we need to assess the degree of ethnocentricity in this largely American literature. Peterson's notion of a 'unitary interest' in growth in urban politics has been described as essentially an abstraction of US urban political economy (Orum 1991). Similarly, Western European observers tend to question how well these theories travel across the Atlantic (Harding 1995). That having been said, pro-growth governance addresses one of the most salient sectors of current local government in the advanced industrialized democracies; that of economic restructuring and growth in the local economy. Thus, although the legal and economic framework for local economic development policies varies across national contexts, the basic problematic – the city's dependency on private capital for its tax base and revenues – remains largely the same.

Also, the elitist nature of this model of governance is another common feature of pro-growth governance. It is often pointed out that pro-growth governance is essentially a strategy to purchase economic growth and prosperity at the expense of democratic and accountable local governance. The business community does not want its plans and requests to be the topic of public debate, and local politicians seem to understand and appreciate this. As a result, pro-growth governance is sometimes caricatured as 'talk and decisions in smoke-filled rooms', with no input or control by other constituencies. Thus, an important instrument of this governance model is a somewhat secluded political process.

Some observers have questioned the unilateral focus on growth and the instruments employed towards that end. There are alternative models of economic development that provide for a more socially embedded economic growth, critics have suggested. One of those critics, David Imbroscio, outlines three such alternative models of economic development: 'entrepreneurial mercantilism', 'community-based economic development' and 'municipal enterprise' (Imbroscio 1997). The general idea is to devise a strategy of economic development that caters not only to the business community but also to the broader community. The potential of these strategies notwithstanding, the basic problem is that many communities facing economic decline are not in a position to define the rules of the game; in the short term they have little choice but to embark on growth strategies, sometimes rather non-discriminatory strategies. The title of the oft-cited article 'Shoot Anything that Flies; Claim Anything that Falls' (Rubin 1988) substantiates the pursuit of almost any source of economic growth.

Other cities can afford to be choosier. Some of the more affluent cities along the Californian coast, for example, have adopted a policy of non-expansion, abandoning economic development and growth as a general urban policy objective, since such a policy is believed to be detrimental to the local environment (Pagano and Bowman 1995). Needless to say, such a policy is not very likely to evolve in declining cities struggling to make ends meet and to deliver decent service to the community. In terms of development strategies, however, it should be noted that non-growth as a policy objective to some extent can be seen as a means to sustain real-estate value and a quality of life. The notion of preserving private wealth, while at the same time catering to the environment, is a powerful political formula in prosperous communities.

Outcomes

Assessing the outcome of pro-growth governance is more difficult than one might first suspect. There is no distinct positive correlation between the amount of resources that a city invests in promoting economic development and the actual economic growth. Many cities and regions that have enjoyed a sustained strong economic development have not been very active in promoting economic growth; their development is instead attributable to a favourable location, a future-oriented business community, or a culture of entrepreneurialism. Conversely, several cities and regions that have had economic growth as a top political priority for decades present a dismal economic development. Political and administrative efforts to boost the economy have not been sufficient to counterbalance the forces of markets or to attract new businesses. Then, of course, there are success stories; cities like Manchester and Liverpool in the UK, Pittsburgh and Cleveland in the US and Gothenburg and Milan in Europe have successfully redefined and modernized the base of their economy. Pittsburgh has transformed itself from the 'steel capital of the world' to a centre for medical research and education; Gothenburg, once dominated by manufacturing industry in the shipbuilding and automobile sectors is today a 'city of events'; Milan has gone from an industrial city to a city of design and art; and so on. Manufacturing businesses are all but gone and have been replaced by hotels, galleries, espresso bars, florists and commercial services. While economic development is essentially man-made, the role of economic development policies in creating growth is more unclear.

However, markets lack a social conscience. While they can bring prosperity to the city, the extent to which that prosperity is distributed to all segments of society is an altogether different issue. The 'trickle-down' philosophy which was used both in the United States and Britain to install some legitimacy for aggressive pro-growth policies has so far proven false; at best, 'a *weak* link exists between local employment growth and the level of unemployment' (Hambleton 1990: 81, italics in original; see also Hausner and Robson 1985); in and of itself, growth does not bring about increased distribution, let alone redistribution. As a result, the economic inequalities that characterized the typical industrial city still live on, albeit for different reasons. The modern, cosmopolitan, service-sector-dominated city displays a dual economy with a middle class enjoying services frequently produced by a minimum wage-earning working class, often overwhelmingly with immigrant background. This was the pattern Saskia Sassen (2001) found to be typical in 'global cities' like New York, London and Tokyo, but the same basic pattern of wealth and job distribution is found in almost any contemporary city.

Thus, the outcomes of pro-growth governance – increased chances of a positive economic development – are not automatically to the benefit of all members of the community.

Needless to say, the extent to which such equality is desirable is a political question beyond this book. What we can say, however, is that if some degree of equality is a political objective, that goal will not be reached by a unitary emphasis on economic growth; it requires some degree of distributive urban policies (some, like Michael Keating, would also say redistributive urban politics: Keating 1991). We will look at such policies in more detail in the next chapter.

Pro-growth governance in perspective

Economic growth has been the unrivalled political priority for the past century or even longer. It has not been until the 1990s and 2000s that other concerns, like environmental protection and global warming or 'quality of life' have emerged as contenders to economic development. Unless you live in the inner parts of Bhutan or on some remote island, your wellbeing is directly or indirectly contingent on the pace of economic growth in the city or country you live in. This applies not only to businessmen and salesmen; it applies equally to artists, writers, athletes, children and academics (Logan and Molotch 1987). The individual dependency on economic growth aggregates into a powerful political force urging politicians to prioritize economic development. Electoral research shows that the economic development during a government's term in office is, under most circumstances, one of the best predictors of the outcome of the election (Anderson 2007).

Is there a political or democratic danger in this focus on growth? If this is what essentially everyone expects from the city leadership, is it not entirely natural for urban governance to pursue those objectives? Well, yes and no. Democracy is a more complex phenomenon than leaders following their voters' wishes and demands. Most of us still commute by car, although at some level we know that it would be better for the environment if we travelled by public transport. Political leadership is not just a matter of following but of leading, even if that should include making decisions which not everyone in the community subscribes to. Economic growth is essential to almost all cities in the world, yet urban political leadership has a responsibility to ensure that the pursuit of growth does not jeopardize the long-term quality of life in the city. This is what sustainable development is all about.

Politically complex as it is, economic growth must thus be weighed against other political goals. Environmental concerns, broadly defined, constitute a significant factor; some degree – how much is a political matter – of economic equality is another. As we have seen in this chapter, there is much evidence that economic growth and urban pro-growth governance do not in and of themselves contribute to economic equality, but rather tend to exacerbate economic inequality. The 'trickle-down' effect, which was heralded in America during the 1980s, turned out to be an illusion. The extent to which increasing inequalities pose a problem to the pro-growth political project has been a debated issue and we will not go into it here. Suffice it to say that sustained, and sustainable, economic growth requires that the political leadership has the capacity to embed the economy in a larger context of social norms and political objectives.

Paul Peterson's notion of a unitary interest in economic growth came under intense attack from urbanists during the 1990s. While it does seem to be the case, as discussed earlier, that almost everyone has a stake in growth, we also see that some actors on the urban political scene choose not to pursue growth policies (Pagano and Bowman 1995). True, some cities can afford the luxury of rejecting economic development, but if we look more broadly at this issue we see that it is linked to the trickle-down philosophy; the extent to which citizens support pro-growth policies depends on the extent to which they share the fruits of that growth. Again, generating wealth and distributing it are two very different sets of issues. Let us now turn to a model of governance which seeks to cater to the losers in the economic-growth game.

Chapter 6

Welfare Governance

The previous chapter looked at urban governance geared to promote economic growth. This chapter offers a quite different view on urban governance; one in which growth is all but non-existent and where the city has a primary role in accommodating its populace in a declining economy. As with all the governance models discussed in this book, the core argument is that the objectives of governance are related to the configuration of actors dominating that governance. Thus, we assume that there is a close linkage between those who control governance and the goals pursued in the process of governance. We should think about urban governance not just as a configuration of actors – in networks, in markets, or in political institutions – but also in terms of the direction and objectives of governance. Those objectives are defined in the tension between what is and what dominant political players think should be. Welfare governance emerges in political and economic contexts where the private sector offers only limited opportunities for work, and where work is available it is primarily low-wage, low-skill jobs. The local economy is declining. The city may once have been a prosperous industrial town but it failed to restructure and modernize when the dominant industries became obsolete. These are the 'welfare cities ... the economic backwaters of the advanced capitalist societies, largely abandoned by private capital, passed over in plans for regional redevelopment, and heavily dependent on governmental spending to maintain individual and collective existence at a subsistence level' (Gurr and King 1987: 200).

Market pressures, although extremely powerful in some countries, have not been able to persuade the laid-off labour to move to find new jobs elsewhere. Instead, it is the public sector that provides the economic base of the city's dwellers, through unemployment support or welfare programmes or social security. The extent to which those programmes are sufficient to sustain the daily life for the largely unemployed people or if they have to relocate to find new means of earning an income depends on the level of support in the programmes.

In welfare-state countries like most northern European states, the public sector through (central government) social insurance programmes and (local government) social welfare provides the individual with a safety net in case of a loss of job. In other countries such safety nets are much weaker, hence the pressure to abandon the declining city is stronger. Today almost all countries, however, tend to place more responsibility on the individual in securing the necessary income to sustain their existence. In the United States, President Clinton, in August 1996, signed a law that urged states to create incentives for, and assist, welfare recipients to find new jobs, a policy known as 'From Welfare to Workfare'. That reform appears to have served as a role model for similar initiatives in other countries, including the advanced welfare states in Europe.

Welfare and economic restructuring

To understand how cities can evolve into this kind of welfare-based economy we must briefly discuss the dynamics of the capitalist economy (see Massey and Meegan 1982). The global economy is characterized by a continuous redefinition of the economic base of nations and cities. In the 1970s, most of the cheap, low-tech commodities were typically manufactured in Japan or Hong Kong. Labour and other production-factor costs there were lower than in the rest of the world. The competitive advantage of Europe and the United States was in more knowledge-intensive sectors, which at that time was in sectors such as automobiles, textiles and shipbuilding. By the 1990s, the economic map of the world was almost completely redrawn. Shipbuilding, steel and textiles in Europe were all but gone, generating massive labour lay-offs. The automobile industry was struggling to keep up with their rapidly growing Japanese competitors. Low-tech products were now mainly manufactured in southern Europe, Taiwan and Latin America. By the early twentieth century, the economic geography had shifted yet again: China and the Baltic states hosted much of low-tech industries; meanwhile, Japan, Korea, parts of the United States and India were leading (or rapidly emerging) powers in high-tech economic ventures; and Europe was reasserting itself as a region basing its economy in high-tech, research-intensive industries. Also, the industrial and agricultural sectors in large parts of the world were declining, giving way to the growing service sector.

Geographer Doreen Massey referred to this development as a changing 'spatial division of labor' (Massey 1995). Her argument, harshly summarized, is that, globally speaking, there is an uneven development in the capitalist economy, which leads to different degrees of competitiveness, or comparative advantage, in different regions of the world. In a related vein, Michael Porter analysed the competitive relationship between countries and changing competitiveness (Porter 1990). At the heart of the process of economic restructuring is, thus, the basic logic of a market-based, capitalist economy which defines competitive advantages among cities, regions and nation states according to factor costs, proximity to markets and to natural resources, and levels of technology (Storper and Walker 1989). This complex cluster of issues, which we cannot do any justice in the present context, highlights the confluence of geographical, political and economic forces of change.

It almost goes without saying that there is very little a city can do to shield itself from these powerful forces of change. They compel cities to restructure and modernize, to the extent that is possible, or to face decline. This presents the city with an agenda it has little choice but to address; as Gottdiener (1987: 15) points out, one of the crises of post-war local government is directly related to 'the profound collapse of manufacturing as the industrial base of the city'. This restructuring is a continuous process; cities that today enjoy a strong, cutting-edge business community in future-oriented sectors of the economy could tomorrow face a deep crisis in their local economy. In the late 1980s and early 1990s, a number of cities jumped on the bandwagon and promoted themselves as 'ICT cities', seeking to attract research and development in information technology. In the eyes of many economic development officials in geographically remote settings, ICT as a strategy of economic development had the unique quality of not being dependent on face-to-face contact between suppliers and customers and could hence be located anywhere. By the mid-1990s, however, the 'ICT bubble' had burst, the industry suffered from massive over-investment, stocks plummeted and many companies went bankrupt.

The good news, from the point of view of the cities, was that the IT sector is far less labour-intensive than the older, larger industries. Even so, however, the IT crisis had ramifications across all aspects of the local economy, including the real-estate market, local consumption and local services. The economic-development officials of those cities were back at the drawing board.

There are many historical examples of these linkages between economic change and the wealth of cities. In the UK, cities like Manchester and Liverpool saw the birth of modern industry. As a result, their economies thrived throughout the nineteenth and a good part of the twentieth century, until some of the Asian countries emerged on the global markets with products which were just as good, if not better, although sold at significantly lower prices. By then, those cities had almost their entire economy tied to manufacturing industry. Shutting down plants and mills essentially eroded the economic base of the city. True, alternative sources of growth could be identified, but the process of bringing them to the city and retraining – to the extent that was possible – those who had lost their jobs in the industry was a slow process. The emerging sectors of growth required skills, which previous industrial workers did not possess. These and many other factors made the process of structural modernization extremely complex and slow. Meanwhile, the city suffered from a failing economy, unemployment, rising crime rate and the emergence of a new social underclass (Wilson 1996).

Some cities have handled the process of restructuring well; others have failed or have simply faced an overwhelming challenge. Manchester and Liverpool are but two examples of big, industrial cities faced with the enormous challenge of restructuring their economies once their core industries had become obsolete. Even a casual visitor to any of these cities can still see the traces of the city's industrial legacy, yet today both cities are 'happening', with regenerated inner cities and a heavy concentration on commerce, service and entertainment. Those who were not able to find employment in this new urban economy are found in the poorer suburbs in the outskirts of the metropolitan regions.

In an intriguing analysis of the linkages between central and local pro-growth strategies in the United States, John Mollenkopf (1983: 40) offers a simple but illuminating typology of cities with regard to their economic history. One type of cities is the old industrial cities, which faced severe problems of economic restructuring and were not able to regenerate the local economy. The second type is cities with a similar background but which were successful in repositioning themselves as administrative or service centres. The third type of cities, finally, comprises 'new' cities – for example, cities in the American southwest – which have experienced an economic boom without having to cater to a legacy of declining industries. Our main interest here is focused on the first type of cities, the once prosperous industrial locales which have not been able to bring in businesses or public organizations to redefine the base of the local economy. Gurr and King (1987: 191–202) take this discussion further by introducing a distinction between passive and active state power and policy on one axis and stagnant vs prosperous (local) market economy on the other. In the resulting two-by-two table, cities embedded in a passive state policy style and that are characterized by a stagnant local economy are labelled 'welfare cities'. A declining and ageing population, a decreasing number of private businesses, low private investment, a deteriorating local tax base and a low level of employment characterize these declining cities.

Governing the welfare city

Welfare governance refers to the governance of this particular type of urban political and economic setting. These cities have very limited viability and growth in the local economy. The main influx of capital into the economy comes through the state (i.e., central government) welfare system. This places these cities in an especially delicate dependency on the state. We have already mentioned the wide range of different state–local relationships in the western democracies, but this plight introduces yet another type of dependency – the secure continuous inflow of funds through different social welfare and social insurance programmes.

Given this dependency on central government spending, this model of governance seeks to include the state to the largest extent possible, as a provider or as an 'enabler', or both. The urban political leadership in welfare governance puts great reliance on the state to provide different compensatory programmes to the city. Indeed, this type of resource mobilization often tends to become more important than trying to reinvigorate the private-business sector, because of the uncertainties involved in such a strategy and also the need to develop networks with the corporate sector, which for political reasons is not seen as an attractive option.

Welfare governance is probably the most politicized of the governance models covered in this book. The industrial legacy of the city coupled with soaring unemployment and frustration with corporate strategies often leads these cities to be politically leftist, sometimes radically leftist. In Western Europe, we find this type of city in former industrial cities in areas such as the Lille region in Belgium, the Ruhr valley in Germany, the Bergslagen region in Sweden, the British Midlands, Merseyside and Clydeside regions. In the United States – where the ideological orientation does not come near the

European mass-political response to the breakdown in the local economy – this type of local economy is typical of the former manufacturing industry-dominated cities of the American 'rustbelt', although a significant number of locales there have been successful in regenerating the local economy (Rodwin and Sazanami 1991).

If the general tenor of the urban political debate, thus, is quite radical, the core constituencies sustaining the dominant political coalition in welfare governance are potentially weak in terms of political capabilities. Its core supporters are frequently equipped with low political self-esteem, often coupled with a critical view on 'politics' and 'the economy', which brought many of the problems they are facing on them. There is often a strong sense, among the recipients of welfare, of receiving the support they are entitled to, and that the state has a responsibility to look after those who were the victims of structural changes in the economy. Recent research suggests that there are quite distinct regional differences with regard to how welfare recipients perceive the welfare and social insurance systems (Olsson 2006). In lagging and rural regions, clients tend to look at different public support programmes as entitlements and the prescribed behaviour is to claim as much as possible. In regions with a stronger entrepreneurial culture and characterized by high growth and low unemployment, on the other hand, welfare and social insurance are regarded much less favourably and are only perceived as a short-term solution. 'Welfare cities' typically express and reproduce the former culture of entitlement; the plight of welfare-receiving families is not their own doing but was inflicted on them by the capitalist economy and it is only fair that the local authority offers them support. What outside observers might interpret as stigmatization and welfare dependencies, these families only see as receiving what is rightfully theirs.

If those are the social norms and prescribed behaviours in welfare governance, the prospect of change would appear to be rather bleak. And, indeed, change is a major problem in welfare governance. The population of the welfare city has seen change and knows what it can mean and therefore there is a tendency to reject change and to hold on to what it has, however insufficient that might be. Also, welfare governance shares the presence of strong organized interests with corporatist governance; neighbourhood organization is often strong and party membership and – to a varying degree, obviously – unionization tend to be high. The extent to which corporatism facilitates or obstructs change in national politics has been a debated issue (Katzenstein 1984, 1985, Olson 1982), and to some extent similar arguments apply to urban governance as well. Critics of corporatism like Mancur Olson argue that it is a model of governance which creates rigidities, since all social constituencies successfully fend off or veto disadvantageous decisions or policies. A case in point would be the rapid decline of the Pittsburgh steel industry; union and management were unable or unwilling to unite behind a reconstruction plan which, temporarily at least, would have prevented plant closure (Hoerr 1988). As a result, a number of cities and townships in the Monongahela valley turned into welfare cities in an amazingly short period of time.

Those who take a more positive view, on the other hand, see corporatism as a governance model where organized interests can legitimize policy and ensure compensations for their members. Supporters of this argument point to the fact that the majority of the smaller industrialized democracies in Europe have a long corporatist history yet have proven capable of continuous adjustment to respond to changes in the international economy.

The particular kind of corporatism we can see in welfare cities, or in urban governance more generally (Hernes and Selvik 1983, Villadsen 1986), resembles these dual features of the role of organized interests, with the difference that welfare governance features are more distinctly defensive in their orientation. They are, thus, not easily mobilized for projects of economic regeneration, and, besides, there is a fair chance that they would not qualify for the new jobs that were to be created. In addition, welfare recipients have few incentives to become involved in urban politics since most of the decisions made are of minor importance to them; their chief concern is that central government's welfare programmes stay in place.

Thus, of the four governance models outlined in this book, welfare governance is in many ways the most challenging from the point of view of local political leadership. The city faces massive economic problems, yet economic development, which should be a top priority, has few significant supporters. A large proportion of the population lives on welfare and social security, yet those programmes are to a large extent beyond the reach of city hall. There is desperate need for inward investment in the local economy, but investors are scared off by social deprivation, low-skilled labour, weak purchasing power, political radicalism and a high crime rate. Creating positive and future-oriented urban governance against this background is a major challenge; indeed, this scenario tells us much about how dependent on social and economic factors such governance is.

If the market thus appears unwilling to provide the economic base for regeneration, the urban political leadership tends to turn to the state for assistance of various kinds. These approaches would typically concern various kinds of public investment to create new jobs in the local economy. They could also request that public-sector institutions are relocated to the city or that the state offers incentives for private-business investment in distressed areas; a policy instrument frequently used in many European countries during the troubled 1970s and 1980s, but which today is quite rare. The main problem with these proposals for state support is that they are not reflective of the state's current views on its responsibilities *vis-à-vis* cities. In the United States, a national urban policy cannot be said to exist any longer. In Scandinavian countries, the pattern is surprisingly similar; it is, on the whole, up to the individual city to define its competitiveness and to pursue those advantages. Sweden is one of very few countries that actively redistributes wealth among local authorities; the so-called 'Robin Hood tax' is a system where local authorities in metropolitan regions receive proportionately smaller state grants than authorities in more remote areas. Except for these few exceptions, the contemporary state is rather reluctant to come to the rescue of declining cities. The central–local relationship remains crucial to the welfare city, however, as it funnels welfare and social security into the local economy.

Welfare governance might appear to be a rather short-term, transient model of urban governance, and sometimes it is; in countries with a low level of welfare support people are obviously more inclined to relocate compared with more generous systems. Pittsburgh, once the 'steel capital' of the world, went through several regeneration campaigns and suffered through the closure of the steel mills in its region – but later emerged as a centre for advanced medical research and was ranked the most 'liveable' city in the United States in the late 1980s. Changes do happen, sometimes surprisingly fast. In the British Midlands, change happened too, albeit more slowly. In Scotland, Glasgow, 'the city that refused to die', had very little going for it once its industry was all but gone, but was able to successfully take control over its development and to embark on a positive trajectory of change. Certainly, massive social problems remain, but Glasgow is considered a model of successful urban regeneration (Hambleton 1990, Keating 1988). Sometimes decline cannot be reversed, as was the case with New Haven, Connecticut, passed over by private investors and overlooked when the highway system redrew the economic map of the US eastern seaboard (Rae 2003).

Objectives

The main objectives of welfare governance are distributive. The dominant political constituencies depend almost entirely on the influx of welfare and social security. Together with urban social services, those programmes are essential to welfare governance.

Can this model of urban governance also be redistributive, that is, give more financial support to the less wealthy by levelling higher taxes or fees on the better-off (Devas 2001)? There has been a debate about the extent to which the city can, and should, engage in redistributive policies (Moore and Booth 1986). Michael Keating (1991) suggests that such policies – or at least policies with that outcome – to some extent already exist. Others are more critical. Paul Peterson (1981) argues that in theory cities can pursue three different kinds of policy: distributive, redistributive and developmental. He is critical towards urban redistributive policies, partly because the local political system and *demos* is simply too small to allow for redistributive policies, and partly because such policies would serve as a powerful disincentive for the middle class to move to the city. In a similar vein, Euchner and McGovern (2003: 26) insist that 'redistributive policies at the local level are suicidal'.

In addition to the distributive objectives, the city's political leaders also have a mission to try to regenerate the local economy. As mentioned earlier, this is no easy task, what with few local entrepreneurs and a weak local market. This plight substantiates the welfare city's dependence on the state, not just the welfare and social security systems but public investment as well.

Instruments

As already pointed out, in welfare governance the relationship with nation state is critical since it provides the bulk of inflow of financial resources. Also, welfare governance is a matter of accommodating critics of the economic system that appears to be the only way to salvage the city's future. Welfare governance often sees a lively civil society and active mass-membership organized interests, protective of their constituencies. While such organizations are generally seen as highly valuable, if not critical, components of urban governance (cf. Clarke 2001), in this particular governance model they to some extent are more part of the problem than of the solution; they are not very likely to offer support to market-based, private-sector-led economic development.

How does a city foster good relationships with the state? The most important issue in this context is how the social and economic situation of the city corresponds with the policy style of the state (Gurr and King 1987). States with a passive policy style have very little to offer cities in decline, almost regardless of the nature and cause of the crisis. Within the confines of that policy context, one important avenue for local politicians to central government can be through party organizations. Such channels may often prove more efficient than the formal, institutional channels. Another, presumably less promising strategy, to develop links to central government can be through national organizations of local authorities. Such organizations play important roles both in lobbying central government and as channels of communication from the political centre to the local level (Pierre 1994, Rhodes 1986). For all these strategies, however, a major problem for the individual city is that it must somehow persuade central government to give it more privileged treatment than other cities, a project that is likely to ignite opposition from those cities.

In sum, welfare governance draws on anti-capitalist sentiments and utilizes networks with higher echelons of government to compensate for the eroded tax base. Apart from these types of inter-governmental contacts, this model of urban governance is the least embracing of the governance models described here; for instance, it is reluctant to enter partnerships with private capital.

Outcomes

The welfare governance model combines a high level of mass political involvement with an aggressive strategy towards private businesses that are seen as the root and cause of the city's plight. The priority given to close contacts with the state – through political or administrative channels – tends to detach or 'disembed' the city from the local economy. This, in turn, may exacerbate the problems in the economy. Moreover, while state subsidies to the city provide some short-term remedy and valuable time to address the economic problems, they easily become addictive to local authorities that see few incentives to try to develop the local tax base as long as the state covers the social costs incurred by the industrial restructuring.

Additionally, the political militancy that these cities display scares off potential private investors (Parkinson 1990). The local political elite's reluctance to enter into dialogue with private businesses is counterproductive to economic regeneration. Thus, the main dilemma in welfare governance is that, while the urban political and economic milieu which fosters such governance is more needy than any other governance model for private investment and market-conforming urban policies, it is at the same time the model of urban governance least equipped for attracting such investment.

The outcomes of welfare governance must be assessed in both a short-term and a long-term perspective. Cities hit by rapid structural change in its economic base can sometimes benefit from the attention such crises usually receive and lobby for extraordinary support measures. Short-term financial support to the laid-off labour and the city-region can help the city address the most acute problems of rising unemployment and increasing social expenditure. However, regenerating the economic base into a more long-term sustainable economy has sometimes proven to be a major problem. Private companies investing in declining cities sometimes do so in order to benefit from tax incentives or other benefits offered to investors, with very little market analysis guiding the investment decisions (Pierre 1989).

In the more long-term perspective, welfare governance is likely to encounter growing economic problems. Unless the vicious circle of weak local market, few investments, increasing taxes, population loss and weaker local market is broken, welfare cities will head towards major problems. The key point here is that welfare cities are not economically sustainable in the longer term, and welfare governance is therefore mainly a transient model of urban governance. Few, if any, central governments accept unconditional commitments to support welfare cities or regions. True, their welfare and social security programmes are targeted not at the city but at individuals, but even here, as we mentioned earlier, there are now stronger financial squeezes on welfare recipients to 'actively seek employment'. This will provide powerful incentives for the unemployed to relocate to where jobs are available and that development will, in turn, provide incentives for the city to engage more strongly in economic development projects.

Welfare governance in perspective

Providing welfare is a key historical responsibility of the local authority. The welfare state, as Montin and Amnå (2000) remind us, is a local (i.e., decentralized) welfare state; it is at this institutional level that services are distributed and where citizens and clients have a face-to-face encounter with social workers.

The 'new conventional wisdom' about cities, as Buck, Gordon, Harding, Turok and their associates put it (Buck et al. 2005), is that cities are increasingly in competition and that their competitiveness, broadly defined, therefore is becoming more and more important. In that perspective, welfare cities have very little going for them. They are potentially hostile to forging partnerships with private capital – Harding's (1998) notion of 'shotgun partnerships' in Liverpool during the early Thatcher years is a telling metaphor of political militancy towards such coalitions in a declining city – and they come with big social expenditures that tend to entail a high tax level. Add to the picture Gurr and King's (1987) observation that some cities are more important to the state than others, and we find that many welfare cities are likely to become stigmatized in decline with little prospect of regeneration and renewal. With less and less commitment to cities in national politics, cities caught in this plight are to a large extent forced to rethink their strategy, or lack of strategy. Welfare governance is not economically sustainable in the longer term; the local economy cannot sustain it and central government does not prioritize supporting declining cities. Over time – as happened in Liverpool – change can come, but at a high price in terms of prestige, pride and politics.

One of the key problems with welfare governance that we have already touched upon is its very limited capacity to organize change, yet change is essential for the long-term economic future of welfare cities. Even in countries with comparatively generous welfare systems there has been a reassessment of the support level. The policy shift 'from welfare to workfare' signifies a political trend towards strengthening incentives for the unemployed to find new jobs, in part by lowering unemployment support. Supporters of the policy argue that most welfare recipients will be able to find a new job. Critics, on the other hand, fear that it will lead many unemployed into poverty. Thus, the heyday of welfare governance appears to be gone; the contemporary state is much less inclined to offer what seems to be eternal economic support to welfare cities. Redefining the objectives of governance from ensuring welfare support to regenerating the local economy and creating new jobs is a major challenge, internally and externally, for this model of urban governance. Engaging the (few) private businesses that exist in the city and embarking on partnerships and campaigns to attract new investment will represent a significant policy shift which significant constituencies on the urban political scene will regard critically.

Interestingly, this development leads towards an urban political economy suggested by scholars from vastly different theoretical models and discourses. One is the model of uneven development. Already in the late 1980s, there was a debate among urbanists concerning what should be the role of the state in relationship to declining cities. It was suggested that the state did not have an unequivocal responsibility to cater for cities and regions that declined as a result of economic structural change. This model of 'uneven development' among cities led to the conclusion that nation states should be more passive in aiding cities in distress, thus creating competition between locales (see Duncan and Goodwin, 1988, Parkinson and Judd 1988). This perspective still looms large in the urban discourse, as we saw earlier (Buck *et al.* 2005).

The other intellectual strand leading towards a similar conclusion is found in public choice theory. Almost half a century ago Charles Tiebout proposed his 'pure theory of local expenditure' (Tiebout 1956), according to which cities should be encouraged to define their niche and their competitiveness and allow individuals to choose where they wanted to live. If someone wanted a high level of social protection and welfare, they should move to cities offering those services. People who preferred low taxes should move to locales offering just that and so on. Competition spurs specialization, which provides individuals with a choice about where to live and what services, and tax levels, to receive. The critique of Tiebout's 'pure theory' aside, there is an interesting convergence between that model, the model of uneven development and the urban policies (or absence thereof) of the contemporary state. Cities, for example in Scandinavian countries, that insisted on increasing autonomy may feel that they received more autonomy than they bargained for.

This means that welfare cities and the model of urban governance that goes with them could well soon be a phenomenon of the past, at least in the western world. The welfare city is closely associated with the industrial city. Large-scale manufacturing is less and less a feature of the European and American economy; we have seen a gradual shift from that type of economy towards a 'post-industrial' service-sector-dominated economy based primarily in small and medium-sized companies. Thus, there is today less likelihood of a large number of jobs disappearing over a short period of time. Furthermore, states on both sides of the Atlantic have adopted a somewhat *laissez-faire* policy style *vis-à-vis* cities. In America, national urban policy is no more. In the UK there is an emphasis on steering by good example, such as 'best practice'. In Scandinavian countries, regional policy has effectively surrendered to market forces; the previous commitment to ensure regional 'balance' in terms of economic development proved too costly for the state to fulfil. In all these different national contexts, the message to local politicians is one and the same: cities must find their own fortunes. This may lead declining cities to cling to welfare programmes, hoping for some change in the economy that could catapult them out of their plight. It could trigger other cities to cross the national border to find strategic partners overseas, as we will discuss in Chapter 8. Or, it may drive some cities to get their proverbial act together and define their competitive edge.

Chapter 7

The Decline of Urban Politics?

There is something mysterious, almost incomprehensible, about urban politics in much of the academic literature, as well as in political debate. Both empirical research and the philosophical, normative discourse on urban politics and local democracy are replete with seemingly contradictory statements and beliefs. Urban politics and local political debate have always been accorded strong positive values and processes of socialization and a school in democracy, from John Stuart Mill and de Tocqueville onwards. But for such debate not to become a meaningless ritual, local political institutions must have some autonomy in relationship to the state and some leverage to steer the local society. If they do not possess those resources, why bother to engage in local politics? Why, critics would ask, should citizens engage in political debate about policy choice when there are no real choices to be made?

Thus, the controversy begins already at the issue of whether there should be autonomous local government in the first place. The scope and freedom of local political choice is obviously a key variable in understanding the significance of urban politics; after all, what would be the logic of having political debate in a city that lacks the capabilities to implement the will of its citizens? The political and administrative roles accorded the city are highly institutionalized and there are very few examples of countries that have radically redefined the role of local government. The 1980s saw a wave of decentralization sweep across Western Europe, alongside the American 'New Federalism', but the core issue of local institutional autonomy in relationship to central government was never addressed. Thus, countries with long traditions in fairly strong, autonomous local government such as Scandinavian countries and Japan still retain that system, just as countries that see local government as 'creatures of the state' – Britain and the United States being two good examples – stick to that principle. That said, where we stand depends on where we sit. In Britain, Labour had a rather mixed view on the virtues of local government while in government prior to the 1979 Conservative electoral victory. Once in opposition, however, Labour became adamant defenders of local government, which they saw as the last stand against the neo-liberal political project launched by the Thatcher government (Magnusson 1996). Similarly, in Japan, local government has from time to time been an important institutional platform for left-wing opposition against the national government (Muramatsu 1997, Steiner *et al.* 1980).

Local government enjoys a much stronger position in Scandinavian countries and Japan, compared to their British and American counterparts. Even there, however, people tend to look with some scepticism at differences in local government services among different municipalities. Such differences, however, are mere manifestations of local autonomy and different priorities among different municipalities. As the Swedish political scientist and local government expert Jörgen Westerståhl once remarked, 'most people cherish the idea of local autonomy until they see the consequences of it' (Westerståhl 1987). Further along that vein, the predominant, if partially inconsistent, view on the relationship between local autonomy and state control among citizens and local political elites in Sweden is that both are important and both can be defended on normative grounds. Politicians and citizens apparently support the notion of centralized government to facilitate equal standards, as well as local autonomy to adapt public services to variations in local demand.

These aspects of urban politics are important in several ways. One important aspect is that the significance of urban politics is also to a large extent the significance of local governance. There is no perfect overlap between the two, as mentioned earlier, but urban governance – at least the analytical models outlined previously in the book – does require some degree of political, economic and institutional support from the city. If the range and scope of urban politics is quite narrow, urban policy choice will not matter very much to potential governance partners and there will be, therefore, little incentive for them to become involved in the governance process. If, on the other hand, there were real and significant choices present in the urban governance process, we would expect societal actors to be more interested in becoming involved, not least because there is a greater likelihood that some decisions may have ramifications for them. That said, the linkage between urban politics and urban governance deserves some elaboration. Cities emphasizing managerial autonomy and some degree of de-politicization – what we call managerial governance – might be said to be examples of a decline of urban politics since it de facto limits the range of policy choice.

Furthermore, the perceived and actual capabilities of local political institutions are also important because they offer a benchmark for a discussion about the extent to which urban politics has declined. It is intriguing to note that the debate on the decline of urban politics has been much more vivid and extensive in the UK than in Scandinavia. British local government has always been less significant in terms of policy choice and service provision compared to local government in Scandinavian countries. It could, of course, be argued that changes have been more noticeable in Britain than in Denmark, Norway and Sweden, but that is probably not the main explanation of the difference. Instead, while the capabilities in UK local government are controversial and contested (Magnusson 1996, Leach and Percy-Smith 2001) the notion of local autonomy is deeply anchored in Scandinavian political culture.

Also, the decline of the urban politics debate is important because the drivers of that decline may well also drive a decline of urban governance. Are the different models of urban governance covered in this book predicated on some level of urban politics and local policy choice? Or, conversely, can emerging models of urban governance be interpreted as a local response to the decline in urban politics? Is urban governance simply a way to recreate some degree of local political debate in an era where urban politics has largely become a matter of delivering public services and implementing central government programmes, but where the range and scope of local policy choice is all but nonexistent? We will return to these questions later in this chapter.

What, if anything, is declining, and, if so, why?

The argument that there is a decline in urban politics has been raised with some regularity during the post-war period. However, there is considerable ambiguity concerning what is declining and why. Coming from a neo-Marxist-inspired theoretical perspective, Gottdiener bemoans a perceived loss of vitality in urban politics: 'The very heart and soul of local politics has died. A form without content remains. The present shell of politics surrounds a progressively empty center. The democratic life of the polis sucks out through a vacuum at the very core of the city' (Gottdiener 1987: 13). Interestingly, however, neo-Marxists have tended to look quite sceptically at urban politics for some time, the main argument being that local politics is insignificant both in relationship with the state and in relationship with private capital and a capitalist economy. A political economy theory of the decline of urban politics suggests that the increasing competition among cities, nationally and internationally, curtails the urban political debate since anything that boosts the competitive advantage of the city takes precedence over everything that does not (cf. Buck *et al.* 2005). Given these two powerful constraints on local politics one would suspect that there is little to debate in city hall.

Thus, the decline of urban politics argument needs to be specified before it can be assessed. It could, for instance, refer to a shrinking range of policy choice at the local level. Ideally, the urban political debate should be an energetic exchange of arguments about where the city should go and what it should look like in 15 or 20 years' time. But many cities and municipalities do not enjoy the luxury of such choice, some because of their economic plight and others because the constitutional framework of local government does not offer cities much choice in the first place. Many cities have seen globalization emerge as a new restriction on their policy choices, not least in policy areas such as economic development, taxation, education and welfare.

Second, the de facto range of urban policy choice may have shrunk as a consequence of a convergence among the policies and ideologies of the political parties. To some extent, such a development would echo those political philosophers who argue that city politics should not be ideologically charged but should be committed to foster a good city, a good urban landscape and to provide for its citizens. To de Tocqueville, Mills and others, becoming involved in urban governance was the duty of all citizens and an important way of socializing young people into society; it was not to be a battleground for ideologically driven parties. Again, one might want to reflect on the logic of extensive debate and participation in such a consensual setting. Taking this perspective further, empirical studies on local government in the UK in the 1980s indicated that it did not make much difference which of the two major parties was in power in the city (Sharpe and Newton 1984). While this finding could be said to echo de Tocqueville's romanticized image of local democracy and the need for elected leaders to be more concerned with their citizens' wellbeing than with polarized policy choice, it also serves to help explain the purported decline in urban politics. After all, why bother to become engaged and vote if it does not make a difference who is in power?

One could also make the argument that there has been a decline in terms of the scope of local government distributive programmes. In most, if not all, countries, social welfare spending is cut back and taxes are cut. These changes inevitably impact on local government. If we add a shift towards managerial governance in many cities we soon find that the stakes and the potential for making a distinct change in urban politics are not that great. There will be a decline in terms of the intensity in the local political debate.

Also, we must note that there is no universal pattern on this issue. The decline of urban politics has been more noted in the United States than in Europe. In Europe cities were resourceful in the 1990s and were successful in extracting additional resources (political and financial) from the state. The decentralization that began in many European countries in the 1980s (Le Galés 2006, Pierre 1994, Sharpe 1988) continued and has helped facilitate political discourse at the local level.

As this very brief elaboration has shown, the decline of urban politics argument rests on several different foundations. According to some, urban politics is declining – or, even worse, has never been an important locus of political debate – because the city is constrained by policy choice at the national and trans-national levels. A second strand of thinking about urban politics suggests that to some extent urban politics should not, normatively speaking, be an arena of fierce political debate. Urban politics is about finding solutions to the problems facing the urban populace, and political ideology should not interfere in the dialogue between elected and electors. Ideologies, in this view, reflect different overarching political objectives on issues above and beyond the urban political space and may thus be a source of unwanted conflict at the urban political scene. De Tocqueville's praise of the consensual and result-oriented town-hall meetings in the United States in the late nineteenth century is a good illustration of this perspective on urban politics.

According to a third group of observers, urban politics is declining because cities are invariably subordinate to economic forces which effectively define the pre-conditions for urban policy choice. Such choice, in this perspective, can hardly be said to exist. And, as we discussed in the previous chapter, even when policy choice is believed to exist, there is a tendency to forget that politicians choose frequently pro-growth policies instead of distributive policies or policies aimed at preserving the environment. Pro-growth policies are far from always manifestations of the omnipotence of the market; they are often outcomes of policy choice. As Harvey Molotch argues, 'cities pursued growth not because they had to, but because those who controlled their politics used them for this purpose' (Molotch 1990: 176). Politicians, and cities, depend on growth and therefore pursue policies to that end. By the same token, policies emphasizing distribution (see Chapter 6) are not always reflections of policy choice; they are dictated by severe social problems in the city. There is a myth in much of the urban politics literature that the more policy choice there is, the more enlightened and socially sustainable the policies. That is, at best, an empirical question which is yet to be tested systematically.

The fourth strand in the debate argues that urban politics is declining because politics at all institutional levels is declining. The financially troublesome 1990s in many western countries seem to have limited the range of policy choice and may possibly also have driven a convergence in the party system. 'New Labour' in Britain and the more pragmatic Scandinavian Social Democracy are cases in point of such a convergence. If indeed the range of policy choice and of the political debate has narrowed at the national level, we should only expect the same development to characterize urban politics.

Finally, a decline of urban politics could be attributable to a decline in participation in political parties and their organizations. There is a fair amount of empirical support for this argument (see, for instance, Katz and Mair 1992). As we will discuss later in this chapter, the cast of actors in urban politics is changing from party mobilization towards single-issue involvement. Such involvement is positive because it sometimes means an avenue into politics for people who would otherwise not be willing to engage in politics. However, from the point of view of the political system it poses a distinct problem, because it undercuts the position of the political parties. And, local democracy is (still) predominantly conducted through the parties and their organizations.

The key problem of assessing to what extent urban politics has declined is thus that it is difficult to separate changes in urban politics from similar or related changes in politics more broadly. If – as we have seen in a large number of countries during the 1980s through to the 2000s – elected governments implement political projects aiming at cutting taxes, shrinking the public sector and reducing the overall scope of the political in society, this will impact both national and urban politics (cf. Maier 1987). It therefore makes more sense to look at a couple of significant transformations of urban politics than to try to assess to what extent there is a decline of urban politics *per se*. In the following sections we will discuss two such transformations: a change in the cast of actors on the urban political scene and changes in the urban political agenda. By necessity, both these transformations will be painted with fairly broad brushes, acknowledging important variations among different countries.

Decline or change?

What if we have been asking the wrong question so far? Could it be that we are confusing decline with change? Is it possible that what is actually declining is the traditional model of urban politics and that there are new types of politics, involvement, issues and arenas that we have overlooked and therefore come to a conclusion that there are a number of factors driving a decline in urban politics?

As we argued earlier, parts of the decline thesis depart from an image of urban politics which perhaps never existed. The scope and range of urban policy choice has always been severely restricted by forces in the urban political economy, by national politics and by the constitutional arrangements pertaining to local government which see it as 'a creature of the state' that is only allowed to do what national parliament has told it to do (Dillon's Rule in the United States and the *ultra vires* principle in Britain; see Gurr and King 1987). True, there is a long history of idealized models of local democracy where the city dwellers among themselves decide on common matters and the affairs of the city, but those days are long gone. But it would be a mistake to take this as proof of indifference among citizens about the city they live in. Take, for example, the 'Reclaim the Streets' movement in several cities in Europe. Often dismissed as a loose network of anarchic troublemakers, these groups in fact present a protest against a loss of public ownership of the urban space to shopping centres, conference facilities and traffic (Kohn 2004). Or, consider the debates in the media that often tend to emerge whenever a city announces a major building or renewal project. Inexpensive and safe housing and residential areas and an open, accessible urban space are essential to the people in a city. It could well be that seemingly few people are continuously engaged in these issues because there is a perception that participation is not worthwhile, given the huge financial stakes and subsequently powerful actors and interests that are involved.

Let us explore the argument that we are looking at dated casts of actors, arenas and issues and that there are, in fact, signs of a new mode of involvement in the governance of the city.

The transformation of urban politics I: changing actors

Let us first assess the status of the traditional actors on the urban political scene. It is sometimes argued that there is a decline of party politics at the local level. The argument has been more common with regard to the Anglo-American systems than in most of continental Europe or Scandinavia. To a significant extent, the decline in local parties is believed to be a reflection of the decline of parties more broadly (e.g., Katz and Mair 1992; but see Selle and Svåsand 1991). The past two decades have witnessed a rather intense debate among scholars about the extent of the decline, if indeed there is one, and what the likely consequences are of that development. Some observers remind us that we need to distinguish between a decline in support for the traditional parties in the party system on the one hand and decline in support for political parties in general on the other.

However, parties and party systems do change; the past few decades have seen new parties finding their way into parliaments in several countries. The traditional parties change, too, in terms of organizational structure (Katz and Mair 1992), party programmes and policies. Thus, there is some degree of adaptive behaviour among the political parties. Furthermore, and perhaps more importantly, local parties have emerged in large numbers in local government assemblies in a number of countries. In electorates with proportional representation there is usually a lower threshold to local assemblies compared to the national parliament and so it is easier for new parties to gain parliamentary representation locally than nationally. There are also parties that are truly local insofar as they do not run in national elections. In Sweden, such local parties exist in more than half of the municipalities (Nordin and Vikman 2006). Most of them are devoted to some specific issue – for example, a land-use planning issue or protest against closure of a local hospital. Indeed, many of them are difficult to place on a left–right scale (or any scale, for that matter), something which from time to time complicates the process of securing a majority in the local elected assembly. But it seems fair to say that these local parties play an important role in vitalizing the local political debate. They certainly facilitate political involvement, possibly for those who would otherwise not have been involved.

Thus, what we refer to as political parties and party systems are more dynamic and adaptable creatures than is perhaps often understood. The decline in urban politics might in part be attributable to an inability or unwillingness among the parties to change and to address new and emerging issues, or, conversely, it could be that the observer fails to see that the political parties are in fact changing, albeit slowly. Also, going back to our previous discussion about the local democratic process as more consensual and less ideological than national politics, parties in urban governance face the problem of balancing politicization and ideological conflict, which is the historical *raison d'être* of the political parties, on the one hand and the search for compromise and accommodation, which is their purported role in local politics, on the other.

There are also changes in the form of participation in urban governance. Single-issue organizations, not least in the environmental-protection sector, find it easier to attract new members than the traditional political parties. In some cases, such as Greenpeace, this is a form of non-participation – other than paying dues – whereas other types of organizations emphasize involvement and action. Either way, the individual does not have to burden herself with the full programme of a political party but can focus on one issue of overarching concern to the individual. These new forms of political organizations are often less rigid and more informal compared to party organizations, something which helps to make them more attractive.

The obvious downside to this model of political participation is that it offers no gateway to city hall, which remains firmly in the hands of the political parties. Thus, in order to convert public opinion into political decisions, single-issue organizations must have some strategy for engaging political parties to get their issues on the political agenda. Here lies a very real governance problem; organizations driving public opinion but lacking access to the process of governing can generate problems of weak and illegitimate democratic governance.

Sometimes the argument is made that there is a growing inequality among political actors and that this inequality harbours parts of the explanation of a purported decline in urban politics. That may be the case, although it should also be noted that urban politics has always featured significant inequalities among its actors (see Stone 1989). Have these inequalities been exacerbated lately? Globalization and the increasing mobility of capital could lead us towards such a conclusion. In that same context, however, we should also acknowledge the importance of the new arenas for political debate facilitated by the internet. Private websites, chatrooms and blogs have redefined the space for political debate. Certainly, corporate clout still carries a lot of weight in the urban political discourse, but the new modes of engagement in that discourse favour those groups that traditionally have been considered to be the weaker parties. Again, determining what is a decline or increase in inequalities can only be done with some attention to other, parallel processes of change.

Finally, we should also note a growing tendency towards taking political and social protest to the streets. The most conspicuous cases of such protest – in conjunction with the WTO Ministerial conference in Seattle in 1999 and the Global Forum in Naples, the Summit of the Americas in Quebec City and the EU summit in Gothenburg, all in 2001 – are examples of riots not aimed at the city itself but rather pointed at peak summits where issues of global injustice are discussed, or, according to the protesters, ought to have been discussed. Other cases of social protest taken to the streets, such as the riots in several distressed Parisian suburbs or in Nörrebro, Copenhagen, both in 2007, were triggered by major frustration with deteriorating public services and purported police brutality. Both forms of protest are, however, manifestations of alienation and powerlessness among the younger generations. And in both cases there is an impact on the city, both in terms of material losses and also a sense of loss of space for the city dwellers. Interestingly, following the Gothenburg riots there was much rhetoric about need to 'reclaim the city', only this time not by alienated youngsters but by the urban middle class.

The transformation of urban politics II: the changing agenda

Another important ongoing change in urban politics is a reshuffling of the urban political agenda. It is true that some sets of issues are perennial features on that agenda: social services, planning and land use and so on. But since around the beginning of the twenty-first century there have been some more noticeable changes.

One such change in the urban political agenda relates to growing environmental concerns at all levels of the political system, as well as trans-national institutions such as the EU and more *ad hoc* international agreements like Agenda 21, the Kyoto protocol and the Bali agreement. The implementation of environmental policy is a complex process involving decisions and actions at several levels of the domestic political system.

However, some international agreements target sub-national government directly without going through national government. Thus, Agenda 21, which is a blueprint for sustainable development in the twenty-first century, signed in Rio de Janeiro in 1992, draws to a certain extent on direct administrative contacts between international and sub-national institutions as a strategy of addressing issues related to the sustainability of cities. This arrangement thus reshuffles inter-governmental relationships and gives local authorities a clear role in the implementation process, independently of central government. The next chapter discusses the development towards multi-level governance as a feature of the internationalization of the city. In the present discussion we will note that globalization and the growing international embeddedness thus has a distinct impact on the urban political agenda and modus operandi. These processes certainly present powerful challenges for the city, but also opportunities and choices (Savitch and Kantor 2002).

Another rising item on the urban political agenda in most countries, which again is related to international embeddedness, is migration. The influx of refugees into a city presents a major challenge to the city's economy-service delivery, but the specific extent and nature of that challenge varies considerably according to national context. In some countries – the United States being perhaps the best example – foreigners entering the country with an intention to stay are offered quite limited support from the government, the philosophy being that there is no better way to integrate newcomers than to put them in a context where they have to learn a new language, find housing and employment and so on. Other countries, like the Scandinavian countries, take a different approach. Immigrants receive more extensive welfare support, assistance in entering the labour market, training in the new language and frequently also training in their native tongue. Thus, recipient countries tend to employ in a path-dependent fashion the welfare concept that is already in place. There are also significant differences among countries with regard to policies of assimilation or integration and the emphasis on ethnicity.

Despite these differences, however, there appears to be a common pattern insofar as national governments identify cities as the main public-sector actor in the accommodation process. The most obvious manifestation of migration is in the larger cities. In some cases – cities such as Birmingham, Marseille, Paris, Berlin – immigrants have for a long time been an integral facet of the urban scene. For other cities, such as many Scandinavian cities, migration has gradually evolved into a major financial and administrative challenge for the cities. Immigrants tend to concentrate in the few larger cities where they often form cohesive subcultures. Shops selling preferred food items emerge, cultural organizations are formed and over time there might even be a mosque or some other place of worship. These facilities, in turn, attract later generations of immigrants with the result that there will be a strong concentration of immigrants to very few cities. The larger Scandinavian cities today display some 20 per cent or more of their population as either born outside the country or as second-generation immigrants. We will discuss this issue in more detail in Chapter 8.

This development has first-, second- and third-order consequences for the cities. The challenge in terms of service provision is obvious, but there are also more long-term consequences. Arguably one of the major challenges is how to integrate the immigrants into urban governance. Many of them come from countries where politics could have cost them their lives, or where politics is what forced them to leave their country, hence they have little inclination to become politically active once they have resettled. Additionally, many cannot relate to the political process in their new country, organized in an awkward manner and conducted in a language they do not yet master. The end result of all this is that immigrants participate much less in urban affairs than the natives. Instead, many seek reference within their respective ethnic groups and shield themselves from the politics and culture of their new habitat. With a quarter of the city population more or less alienated from the urban political debate and governance process we should perhaps not be very surprised to find indications of a decline of urban politics. This situation is a ticking bomb in terms of the deteriorating quality of the urban political discourse. The only comfort is that over time even the more culturally insulated groups of immigrants tend to open up to their new country, but that does not help cover the losses incurred during the earlier years of relative alienation.

There is an obvious linkage between these two discussions. The changing agenda in urban politics and the changing cast of actors influence each other, and in the case of migration changing actors and changing agenda go hand in hand. The real challenge is mobilizing the wide ethnic variety, which the modern city displays, towards some common objective. In many cases, immigrants' organizations have become involved as partners in urban governance although many of their members still lack the efficacy to become engaged themselves.

Professionalism in city politics

We should also briefly reflect on the consequences of professionalism and managerialism in contemporary politics for the vitality of urban politics. The heyday of layman government at the local level appears to be gone. Most of the senior political positions in the city are today filled with full-time employees. Only in the smaller communities do we find layman-led urban political institutions. The key arguments for having senior politicians employed full time by the city have been, quite simply, that running a modern city is a full-time job and that full-time politicians provide a safeguard against bureaucratic control of the urban policy process. Moreover, since such an arrangement does not alter the traditional channels of electoral accountability, it has been difficult to rally any more powerful arguments against that solution. The only concern that has been raised has been that by putting elected politicians on the city payroll there is a potential danger that they come to share the views of the city administration to a larger extent than those of their constituents.

In a related vein, there has been a debate in the UK and the United States about the pros and cons of elected mayors compared to mayors that are elected by the local elected assembly (Greasely and Stoker 2008). Directly elected mayors are said to create better engagement with the media and the business community and to provide for governance that caters to the entire community (for the UK, see Dhillon 2006; for the US, see Svara 2008). Reforming the mayor's office in this fashion could be seen as a response to the criticism against a city-employed political leadership; it obviously does not change the basic problem but it creates a direct democratic channel between the urban demos and the mayor, which clarifies the democratic mandate of the mayor.

Interestingly, managerial governance poses yet another challenge to the traditional model of the city governed by elected politicians. Such governance, the reader will remember, rests on the idea that politicians should set the long-term goals for the city and then leave professional city managers in charge of the 'operative' sections of the organization. If one of the ideas of having full-time politicians was that only then would politicians be able to balance the influence of the city administration, managerial governance might be seen as a process of bringing the bureaucrat back in through the back door. This is obviously not the idea of managerial governance; politicians are still in control, only now they do not have to get bogged down in administrative routines but can concentrate their efforts on goal definition and engaging the community. It is almost a philosophical issue to what extent a deliberate, politically initiated, redefinition of the role of political officials represents a decline in urban politics. Some would readily argue that managerial governance is an excellent model of urban politics since it provides for professional management in public-service delivery (Moore 1995). At the same time it gives elected officials more time for democratic debate and for meetings with constituents, private businesses and so on. Much of that argument also applies to elected mayors, as we have seen, and there is no inconsistency between that model of leadership and managerial governance; to be sure, the two models of urban leadership are a perfect match.

Taking this avenue of discussion further, these institutional reforms, which from time to time have been said to jeopardize the quality of the local political debate, have most likely helped sustain some level of urban political life. If there indeed has been a decline in urban politics, these reforms have not contributed to that development but rather mitigated the problem. Urban governance in a contemporary city requires full-time leadership. Poor leadership caused by insufficient time and resources does not improve the quality of urban governance. Managerial governance, properly conducted, does not eliminate the leading role of elected politicians. It is only if, or when, managers take a political profile that the problems begin (Rhodes and Wanna 2007).

Concluding discussion: a shrinking urban policy choice

There is much to suggest that there is a shrinking scope of policy choice in contemporary urban politics; cutbacks in the city budgets, globalization, less autonomy in relationship to central government as a result of a tighter budget and responsibility for the delivery of state programmes, major changes in the urban agenda which make choice an academic matter and so on. Maybe there never was much real choice in urban politics, or maybe urban politics is not declining as much as it is changing.

As we conclude this chapter we should revisit the question posed earlier: is urban governance the answer to a decline in urban politics, or is the decline of urban politics also the decline of urban governance? In many ways, a broader and more inclusive model of urban governance could well be a refreshing alternative to participation in the more traditional structures in the urban political process. The four models of urban governance described in this book differ rather significantly with regard to the extent to which they facilitate such involvement. Pro-growth governance and managerial governance both de-emphasize popular involvement, the former because it focuses on peak-level interactions between city hall and the corporate elite in the city – a model of governance which is sensitive to mass political involvement (Swanstrom 1985) – and the latter because it accords substantive influence and autonomy to the city manager. Corporatist governance and welfare governance both emphasize participation and involvement, albeit of a more selective and interest-driven character. Thus, all four models designate specific actors or interests a leading position in urban governance and that pattern works against the emergence of new modes of political articulation. That said, the overall governance perspective on urban politics is more open and contextually defined than the more limited government-centric model and in that respect it offers good support for the thesis that governance, in some shape or other, can help resolve a decline of urban politics.

The problem is that all models of governance require a set of urban political institutions as arenas for political debate, as executive instruments and as structures carrying norms and values typical to the city's governance and priorities. From that angle, it appears as if a decline in urban politics will entail also a decline in urban governance. Governance is not a substitute for government but rather a different perspective on the social embeddedness of government.

All of this having been said, however, it should be noted that the urban political process is still very much controlled by the political parties. Local elections and elected assemblies and, therefore, much of the structuring of city policies and politics, are in the hands of the parties and their organizations. This situation becomes more complex in those cases when public political involvement is stirred on some particular issue and single-issue organizations confront the local party system. Thus, what some might see as problems of high levels of involvement others interpret as a sign of vitality in urban politics.

Chapter 8

Cities in Global Governance

The days of ordered institutional hierarchies appear to be gone, perhaps for good. Today, to say that the global, national, regional and local institutional levels are becoming more and more intertwined has become an almost banal statement. Global governance is not only a matter for nation states and trans-national institutions but for cities and regions as well. And, by the same logic, global forces – both political and economic – impact cities more strongly than before, challenging cities to accommodate those pressures and to exploit the opportunities that globalization offers. Policies, programmes and 'protocols' evolve through negotiated relationships among states as well as between all levels of the state and trans-national systems of institutions. Within the European Union, to give an example, member states have seen more than half of their previous domestically controlled legislation being replaced by decisions made by EU bodies.

The problem with globalization is that the observer should be careful not to make either too much or too little of it (see, for instance, Hirst and Thompson 1999, Weiss 1998). Some degree of international exposure has been something which a very large proportion of the world's cities has had to live with for an extensive period of time. To these cities, economic globalization from the 1980s onwards exacerbated and complicated contingencies more than introduced them. Thus, we need to be aware that some elements of globalization are well known to most cities, whereas others are more recent phenomena.

That having been said, one aspect of globalization that can claim some degree of novelty is the relaxation of traditional inter-governmental relationships as well as the relationship between domestic and international institutions. Interestingly, this reshuffling of political authority between the national and the supra-national institutional levels in Europe entails not only problems and challenges but also opportunities for cities and regions to position themselves and to team up with city regions (see Scott 2001) in other countries. Most importantly, the EU early on portrayed itself as a 'Europe of the regions', clearly indicating that the creation of bonds between EU structures and sub-national institutions was a high priority. Therefore, however significant the constitutional and institutional restrictions may be on the city as an institution subordinate to the nation state, cities in this new, relaxed institutional system have found several complex challenges in the form of political pressures from new sources, but also new avenues of action which escape central government intervention and control.

As the observant reader has already understood, this is not a book about global governance. What makes a reflection of global governance relevant to the present analysis of urban governance is precisely that they are intertwined. Urban governance is to some extent shaped by decisions and actions not only at the national but also at the international and global levels. It is this aspect of global governance that we will focus on. In addition, we will discuss the increasing tendency of cities to explore international arenas in pursuit of economic growth and political influence. Thus, the theme of cities in global governance will be separated into two discussions. One concerns the tendency among cities to 'go global', that is, to position themselves in international arenas and markets. We need to understand what drives that process and how cities go about that pursuit. And, we need to look at the local consequences of cities 'going global'; how, for instance, does a city's political leadership justify cutbacks in social services at the same time as they spend the city's money on representation in international trade meetings and expositions? In a somewhat different language, we need to analyse the political and institutional challenges associated with an internationalization strategy.

The other discussion on which this chapter is focused is a mirror image of the first; how does globalization impact the city and its governance? What challenges does globalization pose to a city, or a small municipality? Which new actors and interests enter the urban political scene, or are felt as something to which the city has to relate? True, local internationalization initiatives could be seen as a consequence of globalization, but in this section we are more interested in other manifestations of globalization. For instance, we need to know how traditional processes of urban governance, with their focus on place and local issues, can be sustained in the face of international commitments and expenditures. Are they forced to change, or can city life go on more or less as usual, despite globalization and economic liberalization?

As these introductory comments suggest, we must be cautious not to generalize our argument to cover all cities. Washington DC is exposed to other and more noticeable globalization pressures than, say, Walla Walla, Washington State, USA, and Singapore is far more exposed to global pressures than Sunderland. But Sunderland has seen much of its industry come and go as a result of international competition; meanwhile in Singapore's China Town life goes on pretty much as it has for centuries. Thus, we must see the nuances of and different ways in which globalization influences urban governance. No city escapes globalization, but some cities are more directly exposed to the momentum of a deregulated international economy. Similarly, all cities may have some potential gain from embracing globalization by developing international networks and exploring overseas markets for local businesses, but not all cities will opt to do that.

Globalization has two major manifestations at the urban level (see Simone Gross and Hambleton 2007). One is the increasing mobility of goods, money, services and people; as a result of new global flows, some people in the city decide to move (or are forced to move) and leave the city, while other groups, frequently from other countries, move into the city. A major city like Toronto has a population of which 45 per cent are immigrants to the city (Simone Gross 2007: 86). Needless to say, accommodating and integrating these large groups of immigrants poses a major challenge to the city.

The other manifestation of globalization on the urban level is urbanization. This aspect of globalization is more typical to the developing world than the western world, where globalization mainly took place along with the emergence of the industry-based capitalist economy (Le Galès 2002: 52–7). However, although there is now less of a uniform pattern, many cities in the developed world continue to grow.

Going global: the internationalization of cities

We will begin this discussion with a brief historical exposé. In Europe, as in some other regions of the world, cities and city states preceded nation states. Thus, city states across the continent were the main structure of authority, and when nation states were eventually formed they had to impose their authority on the city states. Cities were, in many ways, 'international' actors already in the Middle Ages. For instance, a number of cities around the Baltic Sea, which are now part of Norway, Germany, Estonia, Denmark and Sweden, formed the Hansa Union in the twelfth century, presumably the first free-trade area ever, covering a territory from Bergen in the west to Novgorod in the east, with trade connections throughout Europe. Therefore, startling as it may sound, one could perhaps argue that the era of nation-state hegemony in Europe – the time-period after the city states and before the European Union – is an interlude in the history of cities forging alliances with other cities, sometimes at great distances.

Industrialization brought with it the first wave of globalization. The logic of producing large numbers of products to exploit an economy of scale could not be sustained by the local market, so private businesses sought to widen their market nationally and, in many cases, internationally. Customs and tariffs regulated international trade but, even so, industrial companies soon learned that their competitors were found across the industrialized world and that they had to match or beat that competition in order to stay in business. The differences between different countries, and subsequently cities, were profound. The Michigan-based automobile manufacturing companies could for a long time rely on the ever-growing demand from the domestic market, whereas automobile makers such as Volvo and Saab in Sweden or Fiat in Italy were forced to explore international markets in order to sell a sufficient number of cars to survive.

Moving yet closer to the present date, cities' international contacts were for a long period of time mainly organized as cultural exchanges with so-called 'sister cities'. Cross-border collaboration did not stretch very far beyond annual or bi-annual meetings. The selection of sister cities was often made in a haphazard way or was based on tradition or personal contacts. While the sister-city institution lives on, its traditional design is becoming outdated. Today, cities are much more strategic about who they wish to collaborate with. Cultural exchange as a deciding factor has given way to carefully planned strategic approaches to cities in other countries, although in fairness it should be mentioned that the sister-city model of international networking seems to be becoming increasingly related to economic development too (Berg and Lindahl 2003). The development towards a more strategic approach to internationalization has been under way for some time, at a high pace (see Hobbs 1994). The idea of embarking on an international strategy of some kind is today considered or implemented by a very large number of countries. In a recent questionnaire study conducted in Japan, Sweden and the United States in 2005, 38 per cent of Swedish local government, 39 per cent of US local governments and 8 per cent of Japanese local governments indicated that forging alliances with local authorities in other countries was a 'very important' strategy.

What drives this process of internationalization? What are the incentives? One important idea behind internationalization is to support the local and regional business community to find new markets. Internationalization thus entails a new role for the city. The logic of internationalization is that city regions develop bonds with city regions in other countries to the benefit of both parties. The basic rationale for such collaboration is that businesses in both city regions can identify new markets for their products and businesses with little experience in overseas trade can explore international markets in a somewhat safer and more controlled way than would otherwise be the case. Thus, the key role of the city in this process becomes that of the broker (Eisinger 1988); the city benefits indirectly from these alliances through a positive development of its business sector, economic growth and, subsequently, tax revenues.

Another reason for exploring overseas contacts could be that cities have grown tired of having to lobby the nation's capital for resources to develop infrastructure or other public services. Recall Gurr and King's (1987) apt observation that some cities are more important to the state than others and it becomes obvious why cities who feel neglected by central government are tempted to look elsewhere for financial resources. In that vein, international networks are one option to help bring foreign investment into the city region that would significantly boost the local economy. Unfair treatment may be perceived or real, and may often have historical and cultural roots. In Japan, Osaka has never fully come to terms with the decision to move the nation's capital from Kyoto to Tokyo and there is a fair amount of rivalry and competition between the two cities (Hill and Fujita 1995). Osakans are convinced that Tokyo uses its position as the political centre of the country to promote its interests, sometimes at the expense of other metropolitan regions in the country. For instance, the Japanese government's policies to use taxes and other instruments to decrease the congestion of the large industrial cities in the country do not affect Tokyo since it is not an industrial city, but they have had a powerful impact on the Osaka economy and that of the surrounding Kansai region. True, the pattern of competition between the capital and major economic centres in the country is not uncommon; consider, for example, the relationship between Sydney (or Melbourne) and Canberra in Australia, between Barcelona and Madrid in Spain, between New York (or Chicago or Los Angeles) and Washington DC in America, or between Toronto (or Vancouver) and Ottawa in Canada.

In Europe, by far the most significant driver of internationalization has been the EU (Berg and Lindahl 2003, Brenner

1999, Denters and Rose 2005, Goldsmith 1993). The process of European integration has entailed cities and regions with new opportunity structures to explore in the new international space which the EU has opened up. With its emphasis on linkages between its own institutions and sub-national institutions in the member states, the EU has in many ways been instrumental in opening up the international arena for European cities. The new international opportunity structure refers less to lobbying Brussels for financial resources and political influence, although that is certainly not irrelevant. Instead, the EU policy system offers several gateways to financial resources that can provide the backbone of a budget for urban or regional regeneration. The evidence available suggests that the EU structural funds, targeting cities and regions – not the member states – as the key beneficiaries, have helped strengthen the regional level in Europe (Smyrl 1997).

Furthermore, in the EU's decision-making process, there are special committees for regions and also for cities which voice the interests of these governance levels. Also, the EU arena offers any number of *ad hoc* initiatives and pre-policy conferences which can be of critical value to cities and regions in a particular context, be that coastal municipalities dependent on fisheries, towns and cities contingent for their economy on declining industries, or cities bidding for elevated status in the field of culture. In all these cases, cities and regions need to be present in the EU arena to seize those opportunities which may be of critical economic significance.

This model of contextually defined, non-hierarchical governance, where trans-national and sub-national institutions engage each other without necessarily considering the nation-state level, is generally referred to as multi-level governance (Bache and Flinders 2004, Hooghe 2001, Hooghe and Marks 2003, Pierre and Peters 2001, Pierre and Stoker 2000, Smith 1997, 2003). In contrast to domestic inter-governmental relationships, multi-level governance is characterized by variation from issue to issue with regard to participants; whether a city becomes involved in a process hinges to a significant extent on political entrepreneurship and an institutional capacity to sieze the opportunity, something which in turn depends on knowledge and information. Also, multi-level governance is a negotiated form of inter-governmental relationship; in this example, the EU does not dictate that a city should implement a programme; instead EU officials negotiate with the city leadership about various aspects of a particular project, including its finances. Again, knowledge about the EU official jargon and terminology is essential to the negotiating city.

And, finally, as already mentioned, multi-level governance is non-hierarchical, which means that cities are not constrained by subordination to central government; this also means, however, that they cannot enjoy the safety of the institutional embeddedness in traditional inter-governmental relationships. Thus, multi-level governance, in which the internationalizing city often needs to operate, not least in Europe, requires knowledge about how the EU system works, information, resources and, not least, presence in the EU arena. Taken together, this makes involvement in these processes a rather costly matter for most cities. The potential gains are considerable, but, unlike the costs, they are quite uncertain.

Becoming involved in EU-controlled governance processes is one type of internationalization project. As mentioned earlier, exploring the possibilities of forging strategically defined bilateral contacts with another city-region is another; the sister-city option is a third strategy. These strategies are in no way mutually exclusive; there is good reason to assume that cities pursuing one type of internationalization project are also active with others. Some cities embrace the international embeddedness that the globalized world offers; others are more tentative and careful. Those cities that choose to 'go global' after having developed a sound strategy and secured the necessary resources to sustain the campaign have a fair chance of gaining access to financial resources and trade contacts that will offer a significant boost in their economy. Meanwhile, those cities that sit on the fence may find themselves lacking the funds to develop their economy. Thus, internationalization can create or exacerbate inequalities among cities in a country. While all governments applaud cities and regions performing well, significant imbalances between different parts of the country pose delicate problems of claims for redistribution from the wealthy to the lagging regions or increasing costs related to labour-market policies. That, in addition to the pattern that city regions that do well in extracting resources from international sources become less inclined to respond to incentives from central government, creates somewhat ambivalent feelings towards sub-national internationalization in the nation's capital.

Savitch and Kantor (2002), analysing in detail the impact of globalization on more than a dozen European and American cities, emphasize the need to differentiate among cities in these respects. Cities with an open economy, that is, with a high proportion of their economy based in export-related industries, are obviously more susceptible to fluctuations in market prices and the emergence of new technologies. Furthermore, internationalization is not a strategy that fits all cities. Potential revenues from international projects vary considerably owing to the configuration of the local economy.

Big cities, small countries

The potential gains and losses of internationalization are not only related to the structure of the local economy. They can also be related to the place of the city in the national context. Some countries, such as Japan, Germany, Italy and the United States, display some degree of balance in terms of the size of their cities, whereas other countries are clearly centred around their respective capitals. For examples of the latter category, consider, for instance, Vienna in Austria, Helsinki in Finland and Copenhagen in Denmark, not to mention city states like Monaco and Singapore. These are fairly small countries with a large, international capital; a very high proportion of the country's population lives in the capital. Clearly, internationalization of a dominant capital is a very different (and much more likely) project compared to a similar project contemplated by a smaller city in the same country. We would be less surprised to see a city in Japan, Germany or the United States (Fry *et al.* 1989, Kresl and Fry 2005) embark on internationalization strategies than, say, Tampere, Salzburg or Aarhus.

The centrality of the nation's capital thus produces a centripetal force that does not completely preclude internationalization also by other cities, but certainly means that it poses a bigger challenge. A capital is the country's shop window to the world and the government has strong incentives to prioritize it when it comes to allocating resources among its cities (Gurr and King 1987). The empirical data quoted earlier about the large percentage of cities in Japan, Sweden and the United States perceiving international contacts as very important suggest that perhaps the capital is losing some of its grip on the other cities in the country. In Japan, central government could for a long time rely on subsidies and incentives to ensure compliance by prefectures and cities. With budgetary cutbacks and an economy doing less well than before, Tokyo has embarked on a project of decentralization and merger of municipalities to strengthen local authorities. However, those local authorities have thus become more self-reliant in financial terms, something that could explain a growing interest in internationalization. In the United States, a national urban policy all but disappeared around 1990 (see Chapter 9), again triggering urban strategies to explore other sources of revenue than the federal government. And in Sweden, finally, the EU membership has been instrumental in driving internationalization (Berg and Lindahl 2003).

Urban governance in a globalized world

Let us now change perspective on the internationalization of the city and focus on its impact on urban governance. What does globalization mean to the governing of a city? How, if at all, can urban governance assist in the mitigation and accommodation of global political and economic pressures? What problems do internationalization projects pose to urban governance and the city's political leadership (Keil 1998, Sellers 2001, Smith 1995)?

There is not very much a city can do to assist a private company facing bankruptcy caused by international competition. The history of economic restructuring is replete with examples of private enterprise going out of business, leaving behind communities in decay and decline and with a dissolving social fabric (see Hoerr 1988). Chapter 6 was devoted to an analysis of the ramifications of such traumatic change on a city and its governance. To be sure, the full thrust of a market economy has proven too strong to sustain both for cities and national governments; the era of nation states coming to the rescue of declining companies is clearly over.

Instead, urban governance – particularly pro-growth governance – can make a difference with respect to the pursuit of attracting future-oriented businesses to the city. If a city cannot resist the powers of a globalized economy it appears as if it has little choice but to learn to go with the proverbial flow and to capitalize on the opportunities it offers. For example, a city that can transform its economic base so that it lies predominantly in the service sector may be able to shield itself somewhat against global pressures. The local service sector tends to be less exposed to global economic pressures as such businesses operate to a very large extent with local customers and overseas businesses find it difficult to make their way into that market. Overall, however, as we mentioned earlier, wealthy cities – for instance, suburbs and commuter towns with a strong tax base – can afford not to consider such policies. Most other cities, however, need to look carefully at their options and the consequences of those options.

Internationalization has become one such option to help catapult the local economy from one of decline to one of growth and future-orientation. But this policy choice has consequences for urban governance, some of which challenge the ways in which the city relates to societal actors. In the EU system, funds are usually allocated with very specific strings attached. For instance, the structural funds rules require cities or regions applying for financial resources to show that there is a functioning public–private partnership in place. True, a city that resents the notion of such a partnership is not forced to create one, but that will disqualify the city from financial support.

Another kind of consequence of internationalization on urban governance refers to the political process of securing the funds necessary for internationalization projects. Such projects have potentially big payoffs but also significant contingencies and uncertain variables. The only thing certain about an internationalization project is the cost. The political problem these projects pose is that they must be weighed against other much more tangible sectors of the local administration and service delivery. For example, how do you politically justify spending a large amount of the city's money on participation in an international exhibition in Shanghai when that same amount would sustain a women's shelter or a children's day-care centre for several months? If internationalization projects become politicized in the urban political debate all it takes is a newspaper photograph of the mayor at a wine tasting in the Dordogne to kill it altogether. It is therefore a major challenge for urban political leadership to explain the necessity of developing international networks to secure the future economy of the city.

Internationalization can also easily increase the fragmentation of local authority. Those projects represent a new type of challenge to the city administration and therefore require that an international division of some kind be created in the local bureaucracy. International divisions typically have more financial discretion than most other segments of the administration and, as all departments and divisions, tend to develop their own subculture, only, in this case, with a distinct international flavour. Also, they often tend to develop a somewhat privileged access to the mayor's office, much to the frustration of line divisions. Add to the picture the international division staff, usually recruited on rather special criteria – language skills, corporate background, experience of working in international settings and so on – and it becomes clear that these divisions can easily become an issue with the city administration.

Conclusions

Hank Savitch and Paul Kantor recently completed an extensive analysis of the internationalization of cities, both in terms of their strategic choices to pursue international arenas and in terms of the impact of globalization on their governance (Savitch and Kantor 2002). They conclude that:

> [C]ities have choices, those choices vary with differential resources, and they are not without constraint. But they are nonetheless choices that can be applied. And most importantly, urban choices are not immutable, but capable of expansion, constriction, and modification ... cities are not mere leaves in the wind of internationalization, but political entities that in many different ways shape economic outcomes. (Savitch and Kantor 2002: 347)

An internationalization strategy could be seen as a one of several different urban responses to globalization. In this chapter we have separated the 'defensive' side of globalization – its impact on urban governance – from the 'offensive' dimension of globalization, that is, the opportunity structure which it offers cities (Le Galès and Harding 1998). Few cities escape the pressures of globalization, and the powers of a deregulated international capitalist economy is far beyond that of any city, but the process of defining 'offensive' responses to those pressures does offer choice in terms of strategy and objectives. Is this a city that would like to try to become an international city, or would it prefer to stay somewhat more protected? Would this city be willing to develop international networks or would it rather remain what it is today? The answer to these questions tells us much about the significance of history and shared beliefs and memories in a city.

The inclination among the city's leadership to launch an internationalization strategy depends on the extent to which a political majority in the city perceives such a strategy as necessary and desirable. It also depends on local pre-conditions in terms of financial resources and expertise (Berg and Lindahl 2003,

Savitch and Kantor 2002). There is a pattern of 'Simon says' among cities with regard to internationalization – since other cities do it, so should we – and some observers have been critical towards what is believed to be a fad and fashion among cities to develop international networks and to operate on international arenas without reflecting on whether it is appropriate or feasible to the particular city in question (Beauregard and Pierre 2000). While exploring international arenas is an appropriate choice for some cities, there is a very real danger that other cities follow suit without much reflection as to what they could gain from such an adventure. Internationalization strategies are extraordinarily sensitive to politicization, and it is therefore essential that they deliver tangible results. Here lies a very real problem; 'deliverables' in internationalization projects often tend to be long term and somewhat uncertain.

The EU has opened up almost an 'El Dorado' for member-state cities to explore international arenas. Structural funds have been instrumental in this respect. With the aid of central and regional government, European cities have been able to develop expertise on internationalization in a protected institutional environment. For many of those cities, the structural funds experience may well have been a first step towards a broader strategy of internationalization. But international ventures are not confined to structural funds. The kind of multi-level interactions, which have become a feature of EU governance, have further lowered the threshold for cities and regions to engage with EU institutions for influence on decisions of significance to the city.

The key concept in understanding the preconditions for cities in urban governance is flexibility. In the 1980s Peter Katzenstein (1984, 1985) argued that the reason why the small, European industrialized democracies could handle massive international exposure and competition was that their domestic governance emphasized flexibility. Much of that observation applies to cities in global governance. Global pressures can only be met with a strong capacity to change; there is little comfort in clinging to obsolete economic structures. Similarly, successfully positioning a city in an international arena – for instance, the EU – is a matter of developing an internal capability to identify and exploit opportunity. Unlike domestic-policy processes, influencing the EU process is, to some degree, a matter of being in the right place at the right time; being present at pre-policy conferences, engaging the Commission, lobbying DG representatives and agencies and so on. Flexibility, somewhat paradoxically, perhaps, requires high-quality leadership. The governance of the internationalized city must take into consideration both the development of organizational capacity and, equally important, the consent among the city's constituencies towards internationalization. 'Going international' can easily become a project of concern only to the urban political elite, but sustaining such a strategy in the longer term depends on the leadership's capacity to get people involved and for them to see internationalization not only as a threat but as an opportunity. This is truly a challenge of urban governance.

Chapter 9

Conclusions: The Future of Urban Politics

Ian Gordon and Nick Buck (2005: 6) recently observed that 'the renewed optimism about cities at the start of the twenty-first century involves a shift from seeing them as essentially problematic residues of nineteenth- and early twentieth-century ways of organizing industrial economies towards the idea that they could again be exciting and creative places to live and work'. What represents a city, the profound meaning, role and function of cities, changes over time and across space. We started this book by emphasizing the economic, social and political role of cities in historical perspective. That role continues to change as a result of economic, social and political 'megatrends'.

This adaptive change is, however, not a mechanical process. There is, for the most part, choice (cf. Savitch and Kantor 2002, Stone 1987, 1989). Cities make choices about how to use the land cleared by disappearing industry. Those cities which have a waterfront convert former shipyards to shopping areas or to up-market residential areas or to open urban spaces. While history provides an abundance of cases where powerful economic interests in dialogue with accommodating political leaders shaped those urban strategic choices, there seems to be a growing interest among citizens to become involved in the process of shaping the urban space.

Where there is choice, there is also an obvious role for political debate and discourse. We have previously recapitulated the discussion among urbanists about the extent to which there is policy choice present in the economic development strategies of the city. It would appear as if contemporary economic development choices are more germane to policy choice than were the choices of a few decades ago, with what appear to be more diverse and small-scale options to choose from compared to the few, big industrial projects that characterized the Fordist era.

Let us pursue this argument a bit further. Anyone who revisits a city after a couple of decades is struck by the amount of change that has taken place, unless, of course, the city in question is a historical city like Athens or Siena or Jerusalem. Cities change and those changes begin with choices. The key problem with those choices, as we have touched upon several times earlier, is that they offer huge economic potential to private businesses, building companies and property developers; opinions among the city's inhabitants often tend to go unnoticed (see Chapter 7). Here lies a fundamental dilemma in urban governance; cities that cater primarily to business interests will alienate core democratic constituencies, whereas cities that prioritize participatory democratic debate about how to develop the city will appear hostile to private capital, which may choose to move to more favourable locales. Financial resources and votes are located at different places in the city and urban governance needs to find some balance between the two. The analytical models of urban governance that have been outlined in this book could be seen as different ways of accommodating democratic debate and economic actors.

To understand urban governance – how a city is governed and the political goals that a city sets for itself – this book has emphasized that we need to think of three related clusters or variables; the cast of actors involved, the goals and objectives, and the institutional arrangements developed to pursue those goals. These three sets of factors continuously influence each other. Unlike many other approaches to urban governance, this model argues that the composition of actors involved in governance depends on, and in turn influences, the direction, the norms and the values of governance. Over time, those norms and values become institutionalized in the political and administrative structures of the city.

This chapter will first summarize the four governance models outlined earlier in this book. Following that, we will discuss the future of urban politics against the backdrop of globalization and its impact on cities and the governability of the modern city.

Summarizing urban governance models

It is not uncommon in the governance literature to see arguments about a 'shift from government to governance'. This is a somewhat misleading perspective since government has not left the process of governing. Instead, the key changes that have been observed in many western democracies have been a broader societal inclusion of a wide variety of actors into the process of governing and a new policy style redefining the role of government in that process. Thus, the main change, as Stoker (1998) points out, is not so much about what governments do but rather to how they do it, and what role they play in governing. Interestingly, comparative analyses of urban governance (or, more narrowly, of local government) suggest that local governments 'differ more in what they govern than in how they govern' (Teune 1995: 16). Thus, the 'governance turn' appears to be primarily related to changes in governance style over time and to a lesser extent a matter of changes in the substantive issues that local governments in different countries are responsible for when observed cross-nationally. From both perspectives, however, there has not been a distinct 'shift' from government to governance, but the role of government in governance has certainly changed.

Theories of urban governance stipulate that the role of local government in urban governance is a function of sectoral features; local economic development accords different roles to local organizations than do, for instance, policy areas such as housing, social work, or public transportation. From the outline of different models of urban governance we can see that local government plays significantly different roles in these different models. We will now look more closely at this aspect of urban governance by revisiting the model outlined in Chapter 2. This analysis proceeds in three steps. First, we look at the role of the city in urban governance, specifically studying financing, regulating, mediating, coordinating and monitoring. We then summarize the four models of urban governance with regard to their key characteristics and features. Finally, we look at the four models through the lens of institutional theory, as outlined in Chapter 2.

Let us first look at the roles of urban political institutions in local governance. Table 9.1 gives a summary of the four governance models.

In managerial governance, the city generates the financial resources for urban services from the local tax base. It also regulates the conditions under which private service producers compete with public businesses when bidding for public contracts. Finally, the city plays a coordinating and monitoring role to ensure that services are actually delivered according to the political decisions specifying the quantity and quality of those services. However, managerial governance aims both at making urban service production and delivery as efficient as possible as well as developing alternative strategies for service production, primarily strategies which include contracting out, privatization, or public–private partnerships. Thus, a key element of managerial governance is the incorporation of private-sector organizations into public-service production.

TABLE 9.1   *Roles of local government in different*
models of urban governance

	Models of urban governance			
Roles of the local government	Managerial	Corporatist	Pro-growth	Welfare
Financing	Yes	Yes	(Yes)	(Yes)
Regulating	Yes	No	Yes	No
Mediating	No	Yes	No	No
Coordinating/ monitoring	Yes	No	Yes	No

Corporatist governance presents a rather different picture. Here, the city finances most of the services delivered. It does not play any regulatory role; corporatist governance could be conceived of as a self-regulating form of governance in which organized interests involved in the production and delivery of services do so at arms-length from local authorities. The key role for the city – and for urban governance more broadly – is to mediate conflicts between different social constituencies and to mobilize resources from higher echelons of government.

Financing pro-growth governance is to some extent a responsibility for the city, but important funds can also be extracted from regional or national public organizations (e.g., to help finance investments in infrastructure), or from the corporate sector (e.g., to finance campaigns marketing the locale nationally and internationally). Pro-growth advocates will typically argue that local development projects are essentially self-financing since they – if successful – will increase the city's tax revenues in the longer term. The trademark of this governance model is the public–private fusion of financial resources for projects aimed at boosting the local economy. Obviously, public-service delivery is of limited significance in this model of urban governance. The regulatory role in pro-growth governance refers primarily to two aspects: first, to adapt local regulatory systems so that they minimize intervention in the corporate sector and, second, to regulate local market competition by defining the basic rules of the game.

In welfare governance, finally, the main source of revenue is the nation state. Financial resources are transferred from the state to the city in a number of different ways. Some resources are funnelled directly to the city, but welfare state programmes targeted at citizens in economic distress also indirectly support the local economy. However, in most welfare states unemployment support is limited to a certain period of time after which the unemployed will have to seek social welfare, which draws mainly on local government funds. Thus, securing financial support from the state is a key strategic concern to the city in welfare governance. Additionally, the city needs to explore opportunities to regenerate the local economy in the longer term, but this is a major challenge due to the weak political support for such projects and the limited competitiveness of the city.

In sum, using a simple taxonomy of local government roles enables us to identify more clearly the different roles of local government organizations in urban governance. This could to some extent be seen as a banal statement; different cities prioritize different goals and these differences in priorities will over time be reflected in the institutional set-up of the city administration. But there is more to the institutional argument. The institutionalization of political priorities becomes a self-reinforcing process; institutions put in place to pursue a particular objective will create and reproduce that objective as a political and social norm, which becomes exceedingly difficult to challenge in political debate.

Urban political features in the four governance models

We can now summarize the key characteristics of the four governance models we have outlined in this book (see Table 9.2).

Managerial governance emphasizes efficiency and political and administrative expediency; some might say that this construction of governance is more that of administration than politics. It is not primarily concerned with the politics of urban governance or with political discourse more broadly. Managing the local authority is a task for professionals and relations with outside societal actors are conducted from that perspective. There is little room for ideology in this model of urban governance; to be sure, ideology could best be described as a nuisance which has to be accommodated in some way or other.

Corporatist governance is about distributive programmes and policies. It is a politically charged type of urban governance where the city serves as an arena for political discourse,

TABLE 9.2   *Characteristics of the four models of urban governance*

	Models of urban governance			
Characteristics	Managerial	Corporatist	Pro-growth	Welfare
Political objectives	Efficiency	Distribution	Growth	Redistribution
Policy style	Pragmatic	Ideological	Pragmatic	Ideological
Political exchange	Consensus	Conflict	Consensus	Conflict
Public–private exchange	Competitive	Concerted	Instrumental	Conflict
City–citizen relationship	Exclusive	Inclusive	Exclusive	Inclusive
Primary contingency	Professionals	Civic leaders	Businesses	The state
Key instruments	Contracts	Deliberations	Partnerships	Networks
Pattern of subordination	Positive	Negative	Positive	Negative
Key evaluative criterion	Efficiency	Participation	Growth	Equity

Note: Adapted from Pierre 1999. The concept of 'subordination' is adapted from Offe (1984: 39), who defines positive subordination as a relationship between the economy and the normative and political-administrative systems in which the latter contribute to the economy. Negative subordination refers to a political economy in which the state is constrained by the economy and, at the same time, unable to contribute to its ability to function. In the context of local government, Hula (1993: 38) stipulates that local governments are in a position of positive subordination; they are restructuring in ways 'that mobilize types and levels of private resources not normally available to purely public institutions'; in ways 'that shift programme goals toward traditional economic elites'; and in ways 'that may reduce popular control'.

conflict among organized interests and distribution. There is a paradoxical tension among organized interests in their supporting the city and exploiting it at the same time. Corporatist governance emphasizes the city as a manifestation of the local polity and *demos* and as a vehicle of social justice, but its key actors – organized interests – have selective objectives that potentially undermine the political support for the city and its institutions.

Pro-growth governance is essentially about accommodating private capital and bringing it into the process of urban governance. It is a seemingly consensual model of governance, simply because all major constituencies have a vested interest in economic development and because this model of governance is primarily concerned with the creation of wealth, not its distribution.

In some ways, welfare governance offers the most complex picture. It is a model of governance which caters to the political and material interests of the weakest constituency whose perhaps only real resource is their number. In cities dominated by welfare governance, people who are unemployed or on welfare constitute a sufficiently large size of the local electorate to ensure that urban governance is geared to their interests, but their political efficacy and capabilities are limited. Like pro-growth governance, this governance model's chief goal is to extract resources from the environment external to the city, only in this model it is from the nation state, not private businesses.

Almost all cities have some ingredient of all these four models, although one usually occupies a predominant position. There are obvious tensions between the policy goals in the four models of urban governance. The city contains these different models of governance by allowing for a multi-organizational and fragmented structure where different segments of the local authority are enabled to develop different models of governance. Thus, the fragmentation of the local authority is a reflection and effect of the political competition among constituencies supporting the different models of governance. The differences in perspective on urban politics which the four models display suggest that urban 'ungovernability', in part at least, is explained by a conflict or impasse over what should be the city's policy objectives.

As we have argued throughout this book, the city is embedded in a complex political, institutional and economic hierarchy that effectively shapes its manoeuvring space and autonomy.

In order to develop a broader understanding of the forces that shape urban governance we will use this concluding chapter to address two aspects of that embeddedness. One relates to global political and economic change and the insertion of the city into global political processes. We have already touched on this issue several times earlier in the book, but it is important to return to this discussion as we conclude our analysis. The other powerful external influence on urban governance comes from the action and inaction of the state. By concentrating our analysis of the city on its endogenous actors and processes of governing it is easily forgotten that the state to a large extent defines the preconditions of urban governance.

Globalization and the redefinition of the role of the state in relationship to cities are closely related processes. The issue is not primarily about the extent to which globalization has weakened the state, an issue that has been the subject of a heated argument among political scientists (see, for instance, Boyer and Drache 1996, Brenner 2004, Camilleri and Falk 1992, Evans 1997, Hirst and Thompson 1999, Mann 1997, Weiss 1998). Instead, globalization is believed to have urged national governments to embark on a political project aiming at increasing the competitiveness and attractiveness of the nation and its economy in world markets. In order to achieve that goal, cutting back on the national budget and cutting taxes is an important strategy, and that strategy will have ramifications on the urban economy in terms of cuts in state subsidies and grants. Thus, globalization impacts the city both directly, by exposing the local economy to global pressures, and indirectly, through changes in state policy towards cities.

Cities and globalization

Globalization has swept across the world since the 1980s, redefining political authority at all institutional levels. With only slight exaggeration, it seems as if urbanists have problems making head or tail of globalization (see, for instance, Alger 1988, Beauregard 1995, Douglass 1988, Fry *et al.* 1989,

Knight and Gappert 1989, Smith 1995; but see Savitch and
Kantor 2002 and Hambleton and Simone Gross 2007 for bril-
liant analyses of globalization from the urban perspective). To
geographers, globalization appears to pose less of a problem,
possibly because their theories and analyses are less concerned
with formal jurisdictions and institutions (see Scott 1997,
2001). The standard position in the urban politics literature
is that globalization exposes cities to international economic
forces stronger than hitherto; that nation states 'mitigate' those
international pressures; and that globalization has entailed or
exacerbated a hierarchy among, and within, cities. On critical reflection, there is rather little in this position that strikes
the critical reader as distinctly new. Cities have always been
exposed to brutal economic pressures from overseas; the
nation state has always, to a greater or smaller extent, tried to
cushion those pressures; and there has always been a hierarchy among cities in terms of international exposure but also
opportunity.

The 'world city' analysis is not very complicated; there
have always been cities within the hierarchy of cities with
a global more than a national character (Gugler 2004a,
Knox and Taylor 1995). The first city that could claim some
global status was Rome at the height of the Roman Empire.
Some of the once global cities, like Buenos Aires, have disappeared off the map of world cities while others, like Sao
Paolo, have moved closer to global-city status. Instead, it
is all those other cities, the 'non-global cities', that in many
ways are more intriguing, since they should have come under
some pressure to internationalize. Here, it appears as if some
cities were always contingent on changes and developments
in global arenas and markets, while others – arguably the
vast majority of cities – carry on their daily lives, more or less
oblivious to global changes.

That having been said, it is true – as we saw earlier in
this book – that cities and regions are increasingly positioning
themselves internationally, but is not clear to what extent
globalization is the single most important cause of that development; it appears at least as plausible that the explanation is

to be found in changes in domestic institutional, political and economic factors, that is, factors which only remotely can be attributed to globalization.

To some extent, the explanation regarding this somewhat awkward relationship to globalization among urban scholars can probably be attributed to a tradition to see the city as deeply embedded in the hierarchical structure of the state. In Britain and the USA, the two countries that have shaped the urban research agenda for close to a century, cities have very little autonomy and are essentially seen as creatures of the state (Gurr and King 1987). The Western European local government tradition accords more autonomy to cities and therefore tends to see them as systems in their own right, albeit existing in a domestic institutional framework.

For the present analysis, we note that globalization – just like internationalization initiatives – has ramifications for urban governance, but it is impossible to give a more precise estimate of the extent of those ramifications. Some cities are more globally exposed than others; we need only compare cities with large export-oriented industries with towns in rural and agricultural areas to see the differences in global pressures on cities. Also, global competition for investment constitutes a strong incentive to the state to cut subsidies to local government, as we mentioned earlier. However, globalization is a notoriously slippery concept, and the more we put into it the more challenging globalization becomes to the city.

Cities in national politics

One of the most profound changes during the past couple of decades in the preconditions for urban politics has to do with the relationship between the city and the nation state. During the growth of the public sector in the western democracies, the city played an important role in implementing national programmes, primarily in social welfare. Given the saliency of those policies, local government was an integrated partner with the state in delivering public service. That role of local government has become much less pronounced. True, cities in most countries still deliver the bulk of welfare services, but the heyday of welfare expansion is gone. Public policy today is increasingly focused on global competitiveness and economic growth and, although welfare spending remains a major item in most national budgets, there appears to be less political capital to be gained from those policies. There have been cutbacks and major reform in the welfare sector and, as a result, cities today are less integrated with the nation state than they were in the 1980s and 1990s. It is only logical that most national governments today emphasize urban competitiveness and self-reliance.

This pattern is evident in America, where the federal government up until the late 1980s conducted a 'national urban policy', starting as a part of the New Deal programmes, mainly intended to address social problems in the cities. Since then, however, the national urban policy has declined. Around 1990, observers painted a bleak picture of the state of national urban policy (Kaplan and James 1990, Warren 1990). The decline continued during the 1990s and early 2000s and, in 2005, William Barnes of the National League of Cities eloquently summarized the trajectory of decline by saying that 'the era of federal urban policy is, like, way over' (Barnes 2005: 575). Today, the prosperity of cities hinges on their ability to formulate strategies and mobilize resources for their development.

A similar picture can be seen in large parts of Europe. Here, cities have become probably less important to the state in the sense that welfare-state services are no longer as extensive as a few decades ago. In Scandinavian countries, previous political commitments to 'regional balance' – the notion that the state has a responsibility to ensure reasonably balanced economic development in all parts of its territory – have given way to a political stance according to which regions must formulate a strategy for their development which is based in the indigenous strengths of the region. Similarly in Britain, the signal from Whitehall is that local government must take greater responsibility for its future (Buck *et al.* 2005) and urban policy aims to transform local government from a system of service production to one of strategic, purposive and enabling action (Hill 1994, 2000, Leach and Percy-Smith 2001). The general trend is thus that nation states seek to curb public expenditure, deregulate and cut taxes. Support to local government is not a priority in this type of political project.

To put it a slightly different way, the future of a city or region is now much more up to itself than was previously the case; the state has successfully abdicated its responsibilities for a balanced economic development across its territory. During the 1980s and 1990s there was some discussion about the pros and cons of 'uneven development', as we saw earlier in this book; some suggested that it might be logical to allow for different cities to develop at a different pace, with different objectives and different outcomes, and that the state, therefore, should not seek to balance that development among cities or regions. In fact, uneven development has become a policy objective, if not by design, by default. Most governments have significantly reduced their subsidies to cities and regions. There has been a development from 'the politics of uneven development' to 'the un-politics of uneven development'; by not employing political or economic measures to counteract the unevenness caused by the market, central government has implicitly decided to let the 'spatial market' run its course and allow for significant differences in development among cities.

This shift in national policy towards the cities seeks to obscure the fact that cities still matter in a number of important ways to the nation state, just as decisions and actions by national government are critically important to cities. Some time ago, Gurr and King reminded us that some cities are more important than others; we have returned several times in this book to this observation because it offers much in terms of understanding of central–local relations from different perspectives (Gurr and King 1987). However, which specific cities matter at any given time varies a great deal. In the nineteenth century, Glasgow, 'the second city of the Empire', mattered a great deal to London as a shipbuilding industrial city and a gateway to the world. Today, Glasgow is more of a financial burden, dependent on external financial support to continue its regeneration and to support weak social constituencies. As European industry – textiles, shipbuilding, tools, manufacturing industry – lost its international competitiveness, the same cities that had generated the nation's wealth rather suddenly became the nation's biggest problems. The new, future-oriented base of the economy often emerged in other cities than the previously industrial cities, as we discussed earlier, and the cities that mattered most yesterday matter the least today.

All of this boils down to a situation for the city in which its future prosperity to a very large extent hinges on its capacity to create governance which is both democratically responsive and oriented towards economic and social development (see Buck *et al.* 2005). The general theme of this book is that urban governance should be thought of not just as the configuration of a given set of actors or as actors whose preferences are shaped by the institutional framework they operate within. Instead, urban governance is a process with an objective defined at the junction of actors, institutions and economic conditions. The path that the city sets out for itself is the joint outcome of those factors, and the significance of different types of actors depends on the objective towards which the city strives. As the preceding discussion suggests, recent changes in central–local relationships clearly suggest that it is these local factors that play a major part in explaining a city's future.

The future of urban politics

The analysis of the different roles of the contemporary city also tells us something about the future of urban politics. Recent developments in national and urban politics have altered the role of the city's political institutions in urban governance without necessarily reducing the significance of the city as a facilitator of urban governance. It also seems clear that the role of urban politics in the city is undergoing changes, although these will not in and of themselves reduce the significance of urban politics and urban policy choice. The scope and direction of urban politics change over time, and different roles for urban political institutions are emphasized differently, along with dominant political projects such as social welfare, regulation or economic development. But that is a far cry from suggesting that urban politics as a whole is likely to lose all of its importance. Nation states around the world accord vastly different significance to the local level of the political system, ranging from the small, fragmented and rather powerless American municipalities to the politically and financially strong local authorities of Scandinavian countries. These different roles and capabilities of local government reflect institutional choices of the past; choices which, in turn, reflect the nature of the big political projects of the state. The key point here is that the local level of the political system is accorded some significance in all jurisdictions, even in the United States where it is comparatively weak. Coming back to the quote of Lewis Mumford earlier in the book, if cities are 'the prestige symbol for the whole civilization', then civilization will always be manifested in urban structure and institutions. It is impossible to imagine any civilized society without cities, hence urban political debate and deliberation will always play a role in democratic governance.

That having been said, we must also understand that urban politics is a dynamic and contextual phenomenon. The urban political agenda changes continuously, along with changes in the local economy, national politics and decisions and actions made by international institutions like the European Union. We suggested earlier that to some extent the globalization argument regarding cities is overstated; for the vast majority of cities globalization has not had any major impact. In the European Union, however, cities have become players in complex patterns of multi-level governance; EU institutions communicate and negotiate directly with cities and vice versa. In Chapter 8 we discussed more broadly the causes and consequences of cities being inserted in international and global governance. This type of globalization influences the urban politics agenda; internationalization is costly but also potentially rewarding.

The conclusion is that while cities will always be a defining element of civilization, cities will look different, behave differently and their policies will change over time. The roles of cities, too, change, in time and space. As the four governance models show, different cities prioritize different types of policy owing to differences in their economy, their relationship to the nation state and as a result of policy choice.

Urban governance and urban institutions

Throughout this book we have emphasized the interplay between governance theory and institutional theory. That approach helps us understand that urban governance is embedded in and shaped by an institutional arrangement, both in a structural and a normative sense. Urban governance is shaped by clusters of social norms and beliefs about what should be the main targets of the policies of the city. The city and its governance – what the city does, how it mobilizes societal support for its actions, and how it goes about attaining its policy goals – is the outcome of that tripod of organizational structure, governance and social norms and beliefs. Cities emphasizing economic growth will design their institutions towards that objective, just as cities that wish to promote managerial outcomes will shape their organization to that end. In that process, the objectives of urban governance are reproduced by the local authority.

True, there will always be contending views about what ought to be the objectives and organization of governance in the city. The four models outlined in this book are idealized models, not often seen in real-world urban governance. Instead, different segments of the city tend to conduct different types of urban governance; social welfare administration is primarily involved in welfare governance, while the economic development office stresses the need for more growth-oriented programmes and policies. The institutionalization of urban governance is thus confined to a segment of what often appears to be a fragmented city administration. The issue of what the goals of urban governance should be are at the heart of urban political choice and different segments of the city and the city administration tend to embrace different values.

Interpreting the tension between different models of urban governance thus also helps explain problems of governability or what Pierce (1993) calls 'governance gaps' caused by organizational insufficiency and lack of inter-organizational coordination (see Warren *et al.* 1992, Wirt 1974). This is not to suggest that governance is a sectoral rather than a city phenomenon, but it does suggest that intra-organizational tensions concerning what should be the objectives of governance can be an important source of ungovernability of the city.

Another core theme in the book is that the future of cities is increasingly a matter for the city itself; it cannot expect much help either from the state or from larger industrial and corporate players. To meet that challenge, cities need to get their proverbial acts together: engaging in a discussion about what the city should look like in ten, 15 or 20 years' time; formulating a strategy to attain those collective goals; mobilizing resources from all corners of the community in the pursuit of long-term objectives; and exploring political and economic markets beyond the city limits for resources by which to catapult the city into the coming decades. That kind of project cannot be handled by the city administration alone; it requires broad, societal mobilization. In that respect, it is a classic governance challenge. The modern city, therefore, looks rather different from the city described in the literature of the 1970s and 1980s. It is more open, engaging, entrepreneurial and dynamic. It faces a different set of challenges and, therefore, plays a vastly different role in urban governance. To be sure, the city of the twenty-first century is a set of institutions truly involved in urban *governance* in the core meaning of that concept.

References

Aberbach, J. D., R. D. Putnam and B. A. Rockman (1981) *Bureaucrats and Politicians in Western Democracies.* Cambridge, MA: Harvard University Press.

Ackerman, B. and A. Alstott (1999) *The Stakeholder Society.* New Haven, CT: Yale University Press.

Alger, C. (1988) 'Perceiving, Analyzing and Coping with the Local–Global Nexus', *International Social Science Journal* 117: 341–40.

Anderson, C. J. (2007) 'The End of Economic Voting? Contingency Dilemmas and the Limits of Democratic Accountability', *Annual Review of Political Science* 10: 271–96.

Ashford, D. E. (1975) 'Theories of Local Government: Some Comparative Considerations', *Comparative Political Studies* 8: 90–107.

Bache, I. and M. Flinders (eds) (2004) *Multi-level Governance.* Oxford: Oxford University Press.

Barnes, W. R. (2005) 'Beyond Federal Urban Policy', *Urban Affairs Review* 40: 575–89.

Beauregard, R. A. (1995), 'Theorizing the Global-Local Connection', in P. L. Knox and P. J. Taylor (eds), *World Cities in a World-System.* Cambridge, MA: Cambridge University Press, 232–48.

Beauregard, R. A. (1998) 'Public–Private Partnerships as Historical Chameleons: The Case of the United States', in J. Pierre (ed.), *Partnerships in Urban Governance: European and American Experience.* London: Macmillan, 52–70.

Beauregard, R. A. and J. Pierre (2000) 'Disputing the Global: A Sceptical View of Locality-Based International Initiatives', *Policy and Politics* 28: 465–78.

Berg, L. and R. Lindahl (2003) *Kommunal internationalisering: Internationaliseringsprocesser I Västra Götalands kommuner* [Municipal Internationalization: Processes of Internationalization in the West Sweden municipalities]. Gothenburg: Utvärderingsprogrammet Västra Götalandsregionen, report No. 20.

Boyer, R. and D. Drache (eds) (1996) *States Against Markets: The Limits of Globalization.* London and New York: Routledge.

Brenner, N. (1999) 'Globalisation as Reterritorialisation: The Re-scaling of Urban Governance in the European Union', *Urban Studies* 36: 431–51.

Brenner, N. (2004) *New State Spaces: Urban Governance and the Rescaling of Statehood.* Oxford: Oxford University Press.

Buck, N., I. Gordon, A. Harding and I. Turok (eds) (2005) *Changing Cities: Rethinking Urban Competitiveness, Cohesion and Governance.* Basingstoke: Palgrave Macmillan.

Camilleri, J. A. and J. Falk (1992) *The End of Sovereignty.* Cheltenham: Edward Elgar.

Carrithers, D. (1986) 'Montesqieu's Philosophy of History', *Journal of the History of Ideas* 47: 61–80.

Castells, M. (1973) *The Urban Question*. Cambridge, MA: MIT Press.

Clarke, S. E. (1995) 'Institutional Logics and Local Economic Development: A Comparative Analysis of Eight American Cities', *International Journal of Urban and Regional Research* 19: 513–33.

Clarke, S. E. (2001) 'The Prospects for Local Governance: The Roles of Nonprofit Organizations', *Policy Studies Review* 18: 129–45.

Cockburn, C. (1977) *The Local State*. London: Pluto Press.

Coleman, R. (2004) *Reclaiming the Streets: Surveillance, Social Control and the City*. Portland, OR, and Cullompton, Devon: Willan.

Coser, L. A. (1956) *The Functions of Social Conflict*. London: Routledge & Kegan Paul.

Crawford, A. (1999) *The Local Governance of Crime: Appeals to Community and Partnerships*. Oxford: Oxford University Press.

Crawford, A. (2002) *Crime and Insecurity: The Governance of Safety in Europe*. Portland, OR, and Cullompton, Devon: Willan.

Dahl, R. A. (1961) *Who Governs? Democracy and Power in an American City*. New Haven, CT: Yale University Press.

Dalton, R. J. (1996) *Citizen Politics: Public Opinion and Political Parties in Advanced Industrial Democracies*. Chatham, NJ: Chatham House.

Davies, J. S. (2003) 'Partnerships versus Regimes: Explaining Why Regime Theory Cannot Explain Urban Coalitions in the UK', *Journal of Urban Affairs* 25: 253–69.

Davies, J. and D. Imbroscio (eds) (2008) *Theories of Urban Politics,* 2nd edn. London: Sage.

Denters, B. and L. Rose (eds) (2005) *Comparing Local Governance: Trends and Developments*. Basingstoke: Palgrave Macmillan.

Devas, N. (2001) 'Does City Governance Matter for the Urban Poor?', *International Planning Studies* 6: 393–408.

Dhillon, K. (ed) (2006) *Mayors Making a Difference*. London: New Local Government Network.

DiGaetano, A. (2006) 'Creating the Public Domain: Nineteenth-Century Local State Formation in Britain and the United States', *Urban Affairs Review* 41: 427–66.

Douglass, M. (1988) 'The Transnationalization of Urbanization in Japan', *International Journal of Urban and Regional Research* 12: 425–54.

Duncan, S. S. and M. Goodwin (1982) 'The Local State: Functionalism, Autonomy and Class Relations in Cockburn and Saunders', *Political Geography Quarterly* 1: 77–96.

Duncan, S. S. and M. Goodwin (1985) 'The Local State and Local Economic Policy: Why the Fuss?', *Policy and Politics* 13: 227–53.

Duncan, S. S. and M. Goodwin (1988) *The Local State and Uneven Development*. Oxford: Polity Press and Basil Blackwell.

Eisinger, P. K. (1988) *The Rise of the Entrepreneurial State*. Madison, WI: University of Wisconsin Press.

Elder, N., A. H. Thomas and D. Arter (1982) *The Consensual Democracies?: The Government and Politics of the Scandinavian States*. Oxford: Martin Robertson.

Elkin, S. L. (1987) *City and Regime in the American Republic*. Chicago, IL: University of Chicago Press.

Euchner, C. C. and S. J. McGovern (2003) *Urban Policy Reconsidered: Dialogues on the Problems and Prospects of American Cities.* New York and London: Routledge.

Evans, P. (1997) 'The Eclipse of the State? Reflections on Stateness in an Era of Globalization', *World Politics*, 50: 62–87.

Ferman, B. (1996) *Challenging the Growth Machine: Neighborhood Politics in Chicago and Pittsburgh.* Lawrence, KS: University Press of Kansas.

Florida, P. (2002) *The Rise of the Creative Class: And How it's Transforming Work, Leisure, Community and Everyday Life.* New York: Basic.

Fry, E. H., L. H. Radebaugh and P. Soldatos (eds) (1989) *The New International Cities Era: The Global Activities of North American Municipal Governments.* Provo, UH: David M. Kennedy for International Studies, Brigham Young University.

Goldsmith, M. (1992) 'Local Government', *Urban Studies* 29: 393–410.

Goldsmith, M. (1993) 'The Europeanisation of Local Government', *Urban Studies* 30: 683–99.

Gordon, I. and N. H. Buck (2005) 'Cities in the New Conventional Wisdom', in N. H. Buck, I. Gordon, A. Harding and I. Turok (eds), *Changing Cities: Rethinking Urban Competitiveness, Cohesion and Governance.* Basingstoke: Palgrave Macmillan, 1–21.

Gottdiener, M. (1987) *The Decline of Urban Politics.* Beverly Hills and London: Sage.

Greasely, S. and G. Stoker (2008) 'Mayors and Urban Governance: Developing a Facilitative Leadership Style', *Public Administration Review* 68: 722–30.

Gugler, J. (ed.) (2004a) *World Cities Beyond the West: Globalization, Development and Inequality.* Cambridge, MA: Cambridge University Press.

Gugler, J. (2004b) 'Introduction', in J. Gugler (ed), *World Cities Beyond the West: Globalization, Development and Inequality.* Cambridge, MA: Cambridge University Press, 1–26.

Gurr, T. R. and D. S. King (1987) *The State and the City.* London: Macmillan and Chicago, IL: University of Chicago Press.

Hall, P. A. (1988) *Cities of Tomorrow.* Oxford: Basil Blackwell.

Hambleton, R. (1990) *Urban Government in the 1990s.* Bristol: School of Advanced Urban Studies.

Hambleton, R. and J. Simone Gross (eds) (2007) *Governing Cities in a Global Era.* Basingstoke: Palgrave Macmillan.

Harding, A. (1995) 'Elite Theory and Growth Machines', in D. Judge, G. Stokers and H. Wollmann (eds), *Theories of Urban Politics.* London: Sage, 35–53.

Harding, A. (1998) 'Public-Private Partnerships in the UK', in J. Pierre (ed), *Partnerships in Urban Governance: European and American Experience.* London: Macmillan, 71–92.

Hausner, V. A. and B. Robson (1985) *Changing Cities.* London: ESRC.

Hernes, G. and A. Selvik (1983) 'Local Corporatism', in S. Berger (ed.), *Organizing Interests in Western Europe.* Cambridge and New York: Cambridge University Press, 103–19.

Hill, D. M. (1974) *Democratic Theory and Local Government.* London: Allen & Unwin.

Hill, D. M. (1994) *Citizens and Cities: Urban Policy in the 1990s.* London: Harvester Wheatsheaf.

Hill, D. M. (2000) *Urban Policy and Politics in Britain.* Basingstoke: Palgrave Macmillan.

Hill, R. C. (1984a) 'Urban Political Economy: Emergence, Consolidation, and Development', in M. P. Smith (ed.), *Cities in Transformation.* Urban Affairs Annual Reviews 26. Beverly Hills and London: Sage, 123–37.

Hill, R. C. (1984b) 'Economic Crisis and Political Response in the Motor City', in L. Sawyers and W. K. Tabb (eds), *Sunbelt/Snowbelt: Urban Development and Regional Restructuring.* Oxford: Oxford University Press.

Hill, R. C. and K. Fujita (1995) 'Osaka's Tokyo Problem', *International Journal of Urban and Regional Research* 19: 181–93.

Hirst, P. (1994) *Associative Democracy: New Forms of Economic and Social Governance.* Oxford: Polity Press.

Hirst, P. (2000) 'Democracy and Governance', in J. Pierre (ed), *Debating Governance: Authority, Steering, and Democracy.* Oxford: Oxford University Press, 13–35.

Hirst, P. and G. Thompson (1999) *Globalization in Question: The International Economy and the Possibilities of Governance.* Oxford: Polity Press.

Hobbs, H. H. (1994) *City Hall Goes Abroad: The Foreign Policy of Local Politics.* Thousand Oaks, CA, and London: Sage.

Hoerr, J. (1988) *And the Wolf Finally Came: The Decline of the American Steel Industry.* Pittsburgh, PA: University of Pittsburgh Press.

Hood, C. (1995) 'Deprivileging the UK Civil Service in the 1980s: Dream or Reality', in J. Pierre (ed.), *Bureaucracy in the Modern State: An Introduction to Comparative Public Administration.* Cheltenham: Edward Elgar, 92–117.

Hooghe, L. (2001) *Multi-level Governance and European Integration: Governance in Europe.* Lanham, MD: Rowman & Littlefield.

Hooghe, L. and G. Marks (2003) 'Unravelling the Central State, but How?: Types of Multi-level Governance', *American Political Science Review* 97: 233–43.

Hula, R. C. (1993) 'The State Reassessed: The Privatization of Local Politics', in E. G. Goetz and S. E. Clarke (eds), *The New Localism: Comparative Urban Politics in a Global Era.* Newbury Park and London: Sage, 22–45.

Hunter, F. (1953) *Community Power Structure: A Study of Decision Makers.* Chapel Hill, NC: University of North Carolina Press.

Imbroscio, D. L. (1997) *Reconstructing City Politics: Alternative Economic Development and Urban Regimes.* London: Sage.

Jarl, M. (2005) 'Making User-Boards a School in Democracy? Studying Swedish Local Governments', *Scandinavian Political Studies* 28: 277–94.

Jezierki, L. (1990) 'Neighborhoods and Public–Private Partnerships in Pittsburgh', *Urban Affairs Quarterly* 26: 217–49.

John, P. (2008) 'Why Study Urban Politics?', in J. Davies and D. Imbroscio (eds), *Theories of Urban Politics,* 2nd edn. London: Sage, 17–23.

Jones, B. D. (1989) 'Why Weakness is a Strength: Some Thoughts on the Current State of Urban Analysis', *Urban Affairs Quarterly* 25: 30–40.

Jones, B. D. and L. W. Bachelor (1986) *The Sustaining Hand: Community Leadership and Corporate Power.* Lawrence, KS: University Press of Kansas.

Judge, D., G. Stoker and H. Wollmann (eds) (1995) *Theories of Urban Politics.* London: Sage.

Kantor, P. (with S. David) (1988) *The Dependent City.* Glenview, IL: Scott, Foresman & Co.

Kantor, P. and H. V. Savitch (1993) 'Can Politicians Bargain with Business?: A Theoretical and Comparative Perspective on Urban Development', *Urban Affairs Quarterly* 29: 230–55.

Kaplan, M. and F. James (eds) (1990) *The Future of National Urban Policy.* Durham, NC: Duke University Press.

Katz, R. S. and P. Mair (eds) (1992) *Party Organizations: A Data Handbook on Party Organizations in Western Democracies, 1960–1990.* London: Sage.

Katzenstein, P. J. (1984) *Corporatism and Change: Austria, Switzerland, and the Politics of Industry.* Ithaca, NY: Cornell University Press.

Katzenstein, P. J. (1985) *Small States in World Markets: Industrial Policy in Europe.* Ithaca, NY: Cornell University Press.

Keating, M. (1988) *The City that Refused to Die.* Aberdeen: Aberdeen University Press.

Keating, M. (1991) *Comparative Urban Politics.* Cheltenham: Edward Elgar.

Keil, R. (1998) 'Globalization Makes States: Perspectives on Local Governance in the Age of the World City', *Review of International Political Economy* 5: 616–46.

King, D. S. (1987) 'The State, Capital and Urban Change in Britain', in M. P. Smith and J. R. Feagin (eds), *The Capitalist City.* London: Basil Blackwell, 215–36.

Knight, R. V. and G. Gappert (eds) (1989) *Cities in a Global Society.* Urban Affairs Annual Reviews 35. Beverly Hills and London: Sage.

Knox, P. L. and P. J. Taylor (eds) (1995) *World Cities in a World-System.* Cambridge, MA: Cambridge University Press.

Kohn, M. (2004) *Brave New Neighborhoods.* London and New York: Routledge.

Kotler, M. (1969) *Neighborhood Government: The Local Foundation of Political Life.* Indianapolis, IN: Bobbs-Merrill.

Kresl, P. K. and E. H. Fry (2005) *An Urban Response to Internationalization.* Cheltenham: Edward Elgar.

Laffin, M. (1986) *Professionalism and Policy: The Role of Professions in the Central-Local Government Relationship.* Aldershot: Avebury.

Leach, R. and J. Percy-Smith (2001) *Local Governance in Britain.* Basingstoke: Palgrave Macmillan.

Le Galès, P. (2002) *European Cities: Social Conflict and Governance.* Oxford: Oxford University Press.

Le Galés, P. (2006) 'The Ongoing March of Decentralization in the Post Jacobin State', in P. D. Culpepper, P. A. Hall and B. Palier (eds), *Changing France: The Politics that Markets Make.* Basingstoke: Palgrave Macmillan.

Le Galès, P. and A. Harding (1998) 'Cities and States in Europe', *West European Politics* 21: 120–45.

Le Galès, P. and C. Trigilia (2004) 'Conclusions', in C. Crouch *et al.* (eds), *Changing Governance of Local Economies: Responses of European Local Production Systems.* Oxford: Oxford University Press, 331–43.

Lindblom, C. E. (1977) *Politics and Markets.* New York: Basic.

Logan, J. R. and H. L. Molotch (1987) *Urban Fortunes.* Berkeley, CA: University of California Press.

Lowndes, V. (2001) 'Rescuing Aunt Sally: Taking Institutional Theory Seriously in Urban Politics', *Urban Studies* 38: 1953–71.

Lowndes, V. (2008) 'Urban Politics and Institutional Theory', in B. G. Peters, J. Pierre and G. Stoker (eds), *Debating Institutionalism*. Manchester: Manchester University Press, 152–75.

Magnusson, W. (1996) *The Search for Political Space*. Toronto: University of Toronto Press.

Maier, C. S. (1987) 'Introduction', in C. S. Maier (ed.), *Changing Boundaries of the Political*. Cambridge, MA: Cambridge University Press, 1–26.

Mann, M. (1997) 'Has Globalization Ended the Rise and Rise of the Nation State?', *Review of International Political Economy* 4, 477–96.

March, J. G. and J. P. Olsen (1989) *Rediscovering Institutions*. New York: Free Press.

Massey, D. B. (1995) *Spatial Divisions of Labor: Social Structures and the Geography of Production*, 2nd edn. New York: Routledge.

Massey, D. B. and R. A. Meegan (1982) *The Anatomy of Job Loss: The How, Why, and Where of Employment Decline*. London and New York: Methuen.

Migdal, J. S. (2001) *State in Society: Studying how States and Societies Transform and Constitute One Another*. Cambridge, MA: Cambridge University Press.

Migdal, J. S. (ed.) (2004) *Boundaries and Belonging: States and Societies in the Struggle to Shape Identities and Local Practices*. Cambridge, MA: Cambridge University Press.

Mollenkopf, J. H. (1983) *The Contested City*. Princeton, NJ: Princeton University Press.

Molotch, H. L. (1976) 'The City as a Growth Machine', *American Journal of Sociology* 82: 309–55.

Molotch, H. L. (1990) 'Urban Deals in Comparative Perspective', in J. R. Logan and Todd Swanstrom (eds), *Beyond the City Limits*. Philadelphia, PA: Temple University Press, 175–98.

Montin, S. and E. Amnå (2000) 'Local Government Act and Municipal Renewal in Sweden', in E. Amnå and S. Montin (eds), *Towards a New Concept of Local Self-government? Local Government Development in Comparative Perspective*. Oslo: Fagboksforlaget, 157–85.

Moore, C. and S. Booth (1986) 'Urban Policy Contradictions: The Market Versus Redistributive Approaches', *Policy and Politics* 14: 361–87.

Moore, M. H. (1995) *Creating Public Value: Strategic Management in Government*. Cambridge, MA: Harvard University Press.

Mumford, L. (1938) *The Culture of Cities*. New York: Harcourt, Bryce and Co.

Muramatsu, M. (1997) *Local Power in the Japanese State*. Berkeley, CA: University of California Press.

Nalbandian, J. (1991) *Professionalism in Local Government*. San Francisco, CA: Jossey-Bass.

Nalbandian, J. and S. Portillo (2006) 'Introduction: Council-Manager Relations Through the Years', *ICMA Public Management Magazine* 88(6): 6–8.

Neff, D. (2007) 'Local Wireless Networks – A Prerequisite for the Future', *ICMA Public Management Magazine* 89(2): 10–16.

Nordin, M. and U. Vikman (2006) 'Nya lokala partier i Sverige' [New Local Parties in Sweden]. Mimeo. Department of Economics, University of Uppsala.

North, D. C. (1990) *Institutions, Institutional Change and Economic Performance.* Cambridge, MA: Cambridge University Press.

Offe, C. (1984) *Contradictions of the Welfare State.* Cambridge, MA: MIT Press.

Olsen, J. P. (1986) *Organized Democracy.* Oslo: Universitetsforlaget.

Olson, M. (1982) *The Rise and Decline of Nations: Economic Growth, Stagflation, and Social Rigidities.* New Haven, CT: Yale University Press.

Olsson, S. (2006) 'Attityder och Regionala Skillnader i Sjukförsäkringen' [Attitudes and Regional Differences in Health Insurance], in E. Palmer (ed), *Sjukförsäkring: Kulturer och Attityder* [Health Insurance: Cultures and Attitudes]. Stockholm: Försäkringskassan, 585–620.

Orr, M. and V. C. Johnson (2008) 'Power and Local Democracy: Clarence Stone and American Political Science', in M. Orr and V. C. Johnson (eds), *Power in the City: Clarence Stone and the Politics of Inequality.* Lawrence, KS: University Press of Kansas, 1–30.

Orum, A. M. (1991) 'Apprehending the City: The View from Above, Below and Behind', *Urban Affairs Quarterly* 26: 589–609.

Osborne, D. (1988) *Laboratories of Democracy.* Boston, MA: Harvard Business School Press.

Osborne, D. and T. Gaebler (1992) *Reinventing Government.* Reading, MA: Addison-Wesley.

Pagano, M. A. and A. O'M. Bowman (1995) *Cityscapes and Capital: The Politics of Urban Development.* Baltimore, MD: The Johns Hopkins University Press.

Parkinson, M. (1990) 'Leadership and Regeneration in Liverpool: Confusion, Confrontation, or Coalition?', in D. Judd and M. Parkinson (eds), *Leadership and Urban Regeneration.* Urban Affairs Annual Reviews 37. Newbury Park, CA, and London: Sage, 241–57.

Parkinson, M. and D. Judd (1988) 'Urban Revitalization in America and the U.K: The Politics of Uneven Development', in M. Parkinson, B. Foley and D. Judd (eds), *Regenerating the Cities: The UK Crisis and the US Experience.* Manchester: Manchester University Press, 1–8.

Peters, B. G. (1999) *Institutional Theory in Political Science.* London: Pinter.

Peters, B. G. (2001) *The Future of Governing: Four Emerging Models,* 2nd edn. Lawrence, KS: University Press of Kansas.

Peters, B. G. and J. Pierre (1998) 'Governance without Government: Rethinking Public Administration', *Journal of Public Administration Research and Theory* 8: 223–42.

Peters, B. G. and J. Pierre (eds) (2007) *Institutionalism.* London: Sage.

Peterson, P. E. (1979) 'A Unitary Model of Local Taxation and Expenditure Policies in the United States', *British Journal of Political Science* 9(3): 281–314.

Peterson, P. E. (1981) *City Limits.* Chicago, IL: University of Chicago Press.

Pierce, N. R. (1993) *Citistates.* Washington, DC: Seven Locks Press.

Pierre, J. (1989) 'Public–Private Partnerships in Industrial Structural Change: The Case of Shipyard Closures in Sweden', *Statsvetenskaplig Tidskrift*: 200–9.

Pierre, J. (1992a) 'Organized Capital and Local Politics: Local Business Organizations, Public–Private Committees, and Local Government in Sweden', *Urban Affairs Quarterly* 28: 236–57.

Pierre, J. (1992b) *Kommunerna, Näringslivet och Näringspolitiken: Sveriges Lokala Politiska Ekonomier* [Municipalities, Private Business, and Local Industrial Policy: Urban Political Economies in Sweden]. Stockholm: SNS Förlag.

Pierre, J. (1994) *Den Lokala Staten* [The Local State]. Stockholm: Almqvist & Wiksell Förlag.

Pierre, J. (1999) 'Models of Urban Governance: The Institutional Dimension of Urban Politics', *Urban Affairs Review* 34: 372–96.

Pierre, J. (2000) 'Externalities and Relationships: Rethinking the Boundaries of the Public Service', in B. G. Peters and D. J. Savoie (eds), *Governance in the 21st Century: Revitalizing the Public Service*. Montreal and Kingston: McGill-Queen's University Press, 332–57.

Pierre, J. (2005) 'Comparative Urban Governance: Uncovering Complex Causalities', *Urban Affairs Review* 40: 446–62.

Pierre, J. and B. G. Peters (2000) *Governance, Politics and the State*. Basingstoke: Palgrave Macmillan.

Pierre, J. and B. G. Peters (2001) 'Recent Developments in Intergovernmental Relationships: Towards Multi-Level Governance', *Policy and Politics* 29: 131–5.

Pierre, J. and B. G. Peters (2005) *Governing Complex Societies: Trajectories and Scenarios*. Basingstoke: Palgrave Macmillan.

Pierre, J. and G. Stoker (2000) 'Towards Multi-Level Governance', in P. Dunleavy *et al.* (eds), *Developments in British Politics*, 6th edn. Basingstoke: Palgrave Macmillan, 29–46.

Pierre, J., B. G. Peters and G. Stoker (eds) (2008) *Debating Institutionalism*. Manchester: Manchester University Press.

Pollitt, C. (1990) *Managerialism in the Public Service*. Oxford: Basil Blackwell.

Pollitt, C. and G. Bouckaert (2004) *Public Management Reform: A Comparative Analysis*, 2nd edn. Oxford: Oxford University Press.

Polsby, N. W. (1963) *Community Power and Political Theory*. New Haven, CT: Yale University Press.

Porter, M. E. (1990) *The Competitive Advantage of Nations*. New York: Free Press.

Rae, D. W. (2003) *City: Urbanism and its End*. New Haven, CT: Yale University Press.

Rhodes, R. A. W. (1986) *The National World of Local Government*. London: Allen & Unwin.

Rhodes, R. A. W. (1996) 'The New Governance: Governing Without Government', *Political Studies* XLIV: 652–67.

Rhodes, R. A. W. (1997) *Understanding Governance: Policy Networks, Governance, Reflexivity, and Accountability*. Buckingham: Open University Press.

Rhodes, R. and J. Wanna (2007) 'The Limits to Public Value, or Rescuing Responsible Government from the Platonic Guardians', *Australian Journal of Public Administration* 66: 406–21.

Rodwin, L. and H. Sazanami (eds) (1991) *Industrial Change and Regional Economic Transformation*. London: HarperCollins.

Rubin, H. J. (1988) 'Shoot Anything that Flies; Claim Anything that Falls: Conversations with Economic Development Practitioners', *Economic Development Quarterly* 2: 236–51.

Salaff, J. (2004) 'Singapore: Forming the Family for a World City', in J. Gugler (ed.), *World Cities Beyond the West: Globalization, Development and Inequality.* Cambridge, MA: Cambridge University Press, 240–67.

Sassen, S. (2001) *The Global City: New York, London, Tokyo.* Princeton, NJ: Princeton University Press.

Savitch, H. V. (1998) 'The Ecology of Public–Private Partnerships: Europe', in J. Pierre (ed.), *Partnerships in Urban Governance: European and American Experience.* London: Macmillan, 175–86.

Savitch, H. V. and P. Kantor (2002) *Cities in the International Marketplace: The Political Economy of Urban Development in North America and Western Europe.* Princeton, NJ: Princeton University Press.

Savoie, D. (1994) *Thatcher, Reagan, Mulroney: In Search of a New Bureaucracy.* Pittsburgh, NJ: Pittsburgh University Press.

Schattschneider, E. E. (1960) *The Semi-Sovereign People: A Realist's View of Democracy in America.* New York: Farrar & Rinehart.

Scott, A. (ed.) (1997) *The Limits of Globalization.* London: Routledge.

Scott, A. (ed.) (2001) *Global City-Regions.* Oxford: Oxford University Press.

Selle, P. and L. Svåsand (1991) 'Membership in Party Organizations and the Problem of Decline of Parties', *Comparative Political Studies* 23: 459–77.

Sellers, J. M. (2001) *Governing from Below: Urban Regions and the Global Economy.* Cambridge, MA: Cambridge University Press.

Sharpe, L. J. (1988) 'The Growth and Decentralisation of the Modern Democratic State', *European Journal of Political Research* 16: 365–80.

Sharpe, L. J. and K. Newton (1984) *Does Politics Matter?.* Oxford: Clarendon Press.

Simone Gross, J. (2007) 'Diversity and the Democratic Challenge: Governing World Cities', in J. Simone Gross and R. Hambleton (eds), *Governing Cities in a Global Era.* Basingstoke: Palgrave Macmillan, 73–92.

Simone Gross, J. and R. Hambleton (2007) 'Global Trends, Diversity and Local Democracy', in R. Hambleton and J. Simone Gross (eds), *Governing Cities in a Global Era.* Basingstoke: Palgrave Macmillan, 1–13.

Smith, A. (1997) 'Studying Multi-Level Governance: Examples from French Translations of the Structural Funds', *Public Administration* 20: 711–29.

Smith, A. (2003) 'Multi-level Governance: What it is and How it Can be Studied', in B. G. Peters and J. Pierre (eds), *Handbook of Public Administration.* London: Sage, 619–28.

Smith, M. P. (1995) 'The Disappearance of World Cities and the Globalization of Local Politics', in P. L. Knox and P. J. Taylor (eds), *World Cities in a World-System.* Cambridge, MA: Cambridge University Press, 249–66.

Smyrl, M. E. (1997) 'Does European Community Regional Policy Empower the Regions?', *Governance* 10: 287–309.

Soja, E. W. (2000) *Postmodern Geographies: Critical Studies of Cities and Regions.* Oxford: Basil Blackwell.

Steiner, K., E. S. Krauss and S. C. Flanagan (eds) (1980) *Political Opposition and Local Politics in Japan.* Princeton, NJ: Princeton University Press.

Stoker, G. (1995) 'Regime Theory and Urban Politics', in D. Judge, G. Stoker and H. Wollmann (eds), *Theories of Urban Politics.* London: Sage, 54–71.

Stoker, G. (1998) 'Governance as Theory: Five Propositions', *International Social Science Journal* 155: 17–28.

Stoker, G. (ed.) (2000) *The Politics of British Local Governance*. Basingstoke: Palgrave Macmillan.

Stone, C. N. (1987) 'The Study of the Politics of Urban Development', in C. N. Stone and H. T. Sanders (eds), *The Politics of Urban Development*. Lawrence, KS: University Press of Kansas, 3–24.

Stone, C. N. (1989) *Regime Politics: Governing Atlanta, 1946–1988*. Lawrence, KS: University of Kansas Press.

Stone, C. N. (2008) 'Urban Politics Then and Now', in M. Orr and V. C. Johnson (eds), *Power in the City: Clarence Stone and the Politics of Inequality*. Lawrence, KS: University Press of Kansas, 267–316.

Stone, C. N. and H. T. Sanders (eds) (1987) *The Politics of Urban Development*. Lawrence, KS: University Press of Kansas.

Storper, M. and R. Walker (1989) *The Capitalist Imperative: Territory, Technology, and Industrial Growth*. Oxford: Basil Blackwell.

Strömberg, L. and J. Westerståhl (1984) 'The New Swedish Communes: A Summary of Local Government Research'. Gothenburg: Department of Political Science, Research Report 1984: 1.

Suleiman, E. (2003) *Dismantling Democratic States*. Princeton, NJ: Princeton University Press.

Svara, J. (ed.) (2008) *The Facilitative Leader in City Hall*. New York: Routledge.

Swanstrom, T. (1985) *The Crisis of Growth Politics*. Philadelphia, PA: Temple University Press.

Swanstrom, T. (1988) 'Semisovereign Cities: The Politics of Urban Development', *Polity* 21: 83–110.

Swanstrom, T. (1991) 'Beyond Economism: Urban Political Economy and the Postmodern Challenge'. Paper presented at the annual meeting of the American Political Science Association, 28 August–1 September.

Teune, H. (1995) 'Local Government and Democratic Political Development', *Annals of the American Academy of Political and Social Science* 540: 11–23.

Thelen, K. and S. Steinmo (1991) 'Historical Institutionalism in Comparative Politics', in S. Steinmo, K. Thelen and F. Longstreth (eds), *Structuring Politics: Historical Institutionalism in Comparative Analysis*. Cambridge, MA: Cambridge University Press, 1–32.

Thomas, P. G. (1998) 'The Changing Nature of Accountability', in B. G. Peters and D. J. Savoie (eds), *Taking Stock: Assessing Public Sector Reforms*. Montreal: McGill-Queen's University Press, 348–93.

Tiebout, C. (1956) 'A Pure Theory of Local Expenditures', *Journal of Political Economy* 64: 416–24.

Villadsen, S. (1986) 'Local Corporatism?: The Role of Organisations and Local Movements in the Local Welfare State', *Policy and Politics* 14: 247–66.

Vogel, R. K. (1992) *Urban Political Economy*. Gainesville, FL: University Press of Florida.

Waddington, D., K. Jones and C. Critcher (1989) *Flashpoints: Studies in Public Disorder*. London: Routledge.

Warren, R. (1990) 'National Urban Policy and the Local State: Paradoxes of Meaning, Action and Consequences', *Urban Affairs Quarterly* 25: 541–62.

Warren, R., M. S. Rosentraub and L. F. Weschler (1992) 'Building Urban Governance: An Agenda for the 1990s', *Journal of Urban Affairs* 14: 399–422.

Weiss, L. (1998) *The Myth of the Powerless State.* Cambridge, MA: Cambridge University Press.

Westerståhl, J. (1987) *Staten, kommunerna och den kommunala självstyrelsen* [The State, Municipalities and Local Autonomy]. Stockholm: Civildepartementet.

Wilson, W. J. (1996) *When Work Disappears: The World of the New Urban Poor.* New York: Afred A. Knopf.

Wirt, F. (1974) *Power in the City: Decision Making in San Francisco.* Berkeley and Los Angeles, CA: University of California Press.

Index

165